Other Books by Diane Eble

Men in Search of Work
and the Women Who Love Them

Personal Best

Campus Life Guide to Dating

Welcome to High School
(coauthored with Chris Lutes and Kris Bearss)

A LIFE YOU CAN LOVE

A Guide For
DISCOVERING
Your Personal Style and
DESIGNING
Your Life Around It

Diane Eble

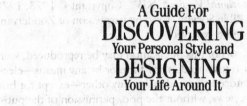

ZondervanPublishingHouse
Grand Rapids, Michigan

A Division of HarperCollinsPublishers

A Life You Can Love
A Guide for Discovering Your Personal Style
and Designing Your Life Around It

Copyright © 1995 by Diane Eble

Requests for information should be addressed to:
  Zondervan Publishing House
  Grand Rapids, Michigan 49530

ISBN: 0-310-49231-9

Edited by Sandra L. Vander Zicht and Mary McCormick
Interior design by Cheryl Van Andel

Printed in the United States of America

ONTENTS

CONTENTS

ACKNOWLEDGMENTS

$\mathscr{I}$ have long been fascinated by both personality and the dynamics of career satisfaction. In this book you have the results not only of my own thoughts and experiences but my years of research in both these areas. I am a writer, not a career counselor. Instead of trying to reinvent the wheel, I have drawn on the material of giants in the field of career counseling to give readers some useful tools that will help them discover their design. This book is, in a way, the essence of what has been most helpful to me as I went about applying the concepts of career development and personality type to the issues that face me as a woman living at the brink of the twenty-first century.

One author who has dramatically influenced me as I searched for my own answers to who I am and how I can best be used in the world is Richard Bolles, author of *What Color Is Your Parachute?* and *The Three Boxes of Life*, among other books. I was still in college when I picked up a copy of *Parachute* and found the exercises enlightening and fascinating. As I continued to follow my interest, I came across the works of others (mentioned in the Resources) who have further helped shape my thinking. And I am grateful to Richard Hagstrom, who helped me define a life-purpose statement.

Janet Penley is another giant I want to acknowledge. Her work in applying personality type and mothering styles has contributed to my ability to develop a satisfying personal mothering style and to pass on some insights to you along these lines. I am grateful to her and to LaVonne Neff for their input regarding material related to personality type, and to the Center for Applications of Psychological Type, Inc., for permission to use some of the material in Appendix A.

I am also grateful to all the women who shared their stories of the struggles they faced and some of the ways they are trying to resolve them.

Lee Ellis, director of Career Pathways, has been a great encouragement to me as well. So have Thom Black, Charlene Baumbich, Betsey Newenhuyse, Janice Long Harris, Andrea Fabry, Bruce Zabel, Curtis Lundgren, and my wonderful editor, Sandy Vander Zicht.

Thanks, Linda Smith, for all those days you volunteered to baby-sit so I could meet one deadline or crisis or another. And thanks to my small group for their support. And to my husband, Gene, who has been unfailingly supportive in my living out a life I can love, I give my deepest appreciation and thanks.

*I*NTRODUCTION:
TORN BETWEEN TWO WORLDS

I am what you might call a two-faced woman, only I don't mean it in the typical sense. I face two worlds, two sets of demands, and sometimes I feel pulled apart by both of them.

One important part of me faces the world of work: I have a career that I love. Like many women, I also need to bring in a paycheck to pay for basic necessities, such as a roof over our heads and the gas to cook our meals. (We're not even talking cars. Our twelve-year-old and our seven-year-old cars run fine for now, thank you; I'll worry about cars tomorrow.) Work is not something I can escape even if I want to. Which I don't, not really . . .

Except that my other "face" looks toward a family I'm crazy about—a wonderful husband, truly a partner, and a son who needs me.

In Search of Superwoman

So here I am, in a bind that I know many other women (and men) face: I have to work somehow (I even want to), but I won't sacrifice my family. Is there a way to do both adequately?

For years I was convinced there isn't. So I put off having children. I didn't want to give up the career I love for raising children.

But I watched. I looked for other women who had found an answer. I read every book I could find on the subject. For a while I believed that maybe it was a simple matter of finding the right help. My husband is and has always been a true partner around the home. If anyone could do it all, according to the books I read about working parents, I thought maybe Gene and I could.

The doubts grew as I observed real-life families juggling the demands of parenthood. My life was already full; in my honest moments I knew there was no way I could add a baby without seriously restructuring my life. I never really believed the superwoman model, that a woman could "have it all"—family, career, community involvement, all at the same time. At least, I knew *I* could never juggle all those roles at the level of excellence I would expect of myself.

I knew that even if I worked full-time, I'd never be able to afford to hire out a lot of work. I knew I wouldn't want someone else to raise my child. And I didn't relish living under a cloud of constant exhaustion.

Eventually, I couldn't put off the decision any longer. Not to decide is to decide, thanks to biology. I'd have to make some choices.

Groping Toward an Answer

I researched every career and life-planning resource I could find. I found that the more I learned about myself, about the way God made me, the more information I had for making decisions that were right for me and my family. I learned why some things are difficult and disagreeable for me (like keeping my files and kitchen cabinets organized). I slowly developed a focus around which I could design my life according to who I am.

I'm convinced that this same process of assessment and seeking options will work for you too.

Maybe you know what you want to do but aren't sure you can do it on your terms. Don't give up. Many women have restructured their jobs to accommodate their personal lives, and the trend is growing.

Maybe you're working because you have to, but you feel dissatisfied with what you're doing. You wonder if there is any way you can feel more fulfilled. Most likely there is.

Maybe you're home with young children, feeling unsatisfied, and wondering why. Or, maybe you're looking ahead to the time when your children will need you less and you can reenter the work force.

Maybe you, like many women, don't really feel you have a "career." You're not sure what will give you a sense of satisfaction. You've held a number of jobs but still don't feel that you have a clear sense of direction. If this describes you, this book will open new doors of opportunity for you.

You won't come up with the same answers I did—that's the beauty of this method. You'll formulate the answers that are right for you. They will come when you look within to your own uniqueness, rather than outwardly to what others have told you that you can or can't do.

How to Use This Book

This book is divided into two parts. Part 1 is a practical tool for discovering what I am calling your "design"—that unique combination of factors that determines where you get your energy, what kind of information you trust, how you make decisions, how you like your world structured, and what special talents you enjoy using. Once you know these things, you can evaluate the tasks and challenges of parenthood and your employment in terms of your strengths and weaknesses. I suggest you get a notebook for working through the suggested exercises in part 1. And because our strengths are best discovered in partnership with others, I strongly urge you to team up with a friend and work through this book, or at least part 1, together.

In part 2 we look at ways to put your design to work in the real world. We'll learn how other women are combining parenthood and employment. You'll see what it takes to make each option work, and weigh it against what you've discovered about yourself in part 1.

A Life by Design

You were born with certain strengths and motivations. Trying to shape your life contrary to this design will make you very unhappy. Knowing it, however, will bring satisfaction and purpose. At the end of your life, you and other people will have a sense of what your life was for. You will have lived by design, not by default.

ART ONE

UNCOVERING YOUR DESIGN

CHAPTER ONE
WOMEN AT THE CROSSROADS

I still don't know what I want to be when I grow up, and I'm thirty-two!" my friend Debra told me half-jokingly. A former elementary school teacher, she had chosen to stay home with her two children until her younger starts school. "I do know I don't want to go back to teaching after my kids go to school, but I don't know what I *do* want."

Laurie did know what she wanted: her career. There was never any question that she would return to work full-time after her baby was born. For one thing, they needed the money (her husband had just finished his master's degree, but there was no good job in sight). For another, she loved her work. To outsiders, Laurie seemed somewhat driven. She held a responsible management position for a publication that she knew was helping change people's lives. She felt a sense of mission about her work.

Yet when her son was born, Laurie was blindsided by the complete change in herself: Suddenly all she wanted to do was have kids—lots of them! Her job no longer held its former appeal. She felt completely bewildered by her feelings.

Andrea's story encapsulates the pull toward both career and family. After ten years in radio, Andrea gave birth to a daughter. She quit her job but was able to work part-time on a fill-in basis, which suited her fine. However, when that opportunity ended, after she had had four children, she felt adrift and guilty. Why wasn't mothering enough to fulfill her? Why did she still feel the need to work? Then an opportunity fell into her lap for a part-time radio job that seemed perfect. After about a year, she got pregnant with her fifth child. Toward the end of that pregnancy, doubts again arose. Could she really do it all?

Do you see yourself in any of these women? For many of us, nurturing and achieving, attending to family and attending to career, developing a personal life and maintaining a career sometimes feel like opposite poles. Is there any way to integrate the two, to combine the two in a way that works for us and our families? Is it really possible to design a life we can love?

The Struggle for Balance

Many of us end up believing that the problem is with us. If only we were more organized, or had more money or fewer children, or whatever, then we'd be able to manage better. I believe, however, that there are very real forces working against the balance we crave.

For one thing, the workplace still operates under the assumption that work legitimately takes up the largest part of a worker's time and energy. I call this the "old male model" because it's based on the assumption that there will be a wife at home to take care of home and children, which circumstance is always seen as secondary to work. If you're part of the workplace, and you have a family, you are caught in a dilemma. Your employer expects your best; you want to please your employer but also give your best to your family. The dilemma is real, and it will be with us until we reshape the workplace to be more family friendly.

In our culture, work done for pay is valued, and work not done for pay is disparaged. Taking care of a home and family is "invisible" labor, work that is devalued by our society. Women (and men) who stay home to raise children, or even who cut back in their career to put the needs of children first, are rarely held up as "successes."

Looking for Answers

Is there an answer to this dilemma of work and family? I believe there is *more than one*.

On a societal scale, I think that we need to do whatever we can to reshape the workplace to be more "family friendly." What this means is finding ways for women and men both to give a realistic amount of energy to work in ways that allow them to also parent effectively. Negotiating for flextime, job sharing, working part-time, starting one's own home business are some possibilities we will explore in part 2. We need to work with passion and excellence, but if we choose to have children we also need to give priority to the awesome responsibility of parenting.

On an individual level, there is no one right answer that fits every woman. Rather, there is a way to go about finding the answer that is right for you, in your situation. There *is* a biblical and workable model, but it is not black and white. God does not give us a blueprint. But he doesn't leave us in the dark, either. He gives us a sense of the direction we are to go, and then he gives us the delightful but frustrating *freedom* to find our own route. And all along the way, he promises to be with us.

The real issue becomes, What is God calling me to do at this point in my life? And the answer is based largely on the gifts he's given you. So the first task is to discover what those gifts are. Then you can go about figuring out how you can best use them, given your particular set of circumstances and needs (which are also from him, if you believe that God is in control of everything).

The first step, then, to finding the right balance in your life between the need to achieve and accomplish, and the pull to nurture and care for others, is to first study how God made you. I call this your design. The concept is based on Ephesians 2:10: "For we are God's workmanship, created in Christ Jesus to do good works, which God has prepared in advance for us to do." God has designed you and me with a unique constellation of preferences, natural abilities, and spiritual gifts to make an impact on this world. In your design you will see patterns—patterns that are uniquely you, patterns that God will want to use for future work.

If you sew, you know that from one basic pattern you can make a variety of different outfits, depending on how you put together the various components. Once you find your own basic pattern, you can design a "wardrobe" of working and caring that fits you and your circumstances. You can create a life you can truly love.

Know Your Design and Kick Out Guilt

Knowing your "design" will also help you with that foe all mothers face whether they work outside the home or not: guilt. Once you grasp how God has designed you, you will begin to clarify a sense of your unique mission in life. Once you find out those two or three particular areas that give you energy, you can use those areas to meet some of your personal and family goals and to express your values.

Let me give you some examples from my own life. Writing and reading are two things I love that never fail to replenish me. Things we love to do, that give us energy, I call "energized skills." They're not just skills we have, but skills we *love* to use. We all have picked up many skills in our lives, but some of them are special. When we use them, we feel energized, alive, at our best.

Writing does that for me. Though it's hard work, and sometimes it's the last thing I feel like doing, there's something about sitting down at the keyboard that pulls me in and energizes me. In a number of ways I have organized my life around this energized ability. Because financially I need to contribute to our household to keep up even a modest standard of living, I write to earn money. I also try to keep a journal to help me achieve personal and spiritual growth. I record our family life, the funny or cute or insightful things my son does and says, the vacations we take, the things that are important to our life as a family. Someday my son will be able to read this and get a flavor of his early life, at least from his mother's perspective.

I use writing to serve the community as well. I write a column for the national newsletter of a mothering group in which I am active. I try to write brief notes of encouragement to friends.

Writing is one of my main means of reaching several of my goals: personal growth, nurturing my family, making a living, and serving the community. No doubt you have many similar goals. In the next chapter we'll start the exciting process of finding out the first part of your design—your personal style.

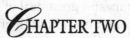

CHAPTER TWO
A PERSONAL STYLE YOU CAN LOVE

A friend of mine designs and makes quilts. She awes me with her ability to take scraps of material and stitch them together to create beautiful patterns. After seeing several of her quilts, I think I am beginning to recognize her style. She gravitates toward cool colors, and diamonds almost always show up in her patterns. My friend's quilts are marked by her own personal style, her own preferences in terms of colors and shapes.

In a similar way, each of us leans toward certain preferences. These tendencies I call *personal style*. We have certain broad preferences in how we think and relate to the world. To know your design and to create a life you can love, you need to know the elements of your personal style. I think of personal style as the "colors" of our design. Just as you are drawn toward certain colors in your clothing and decorating, so you gravitate toward certain preferences in how you deal with the world.

There are numerous ways of looking at personal style. I have found the theory of psychological types the most rich and helpful, because it looks at the way people's minds work rather than simply looking at individual traits. The differences we can see in people make a great deal of sense once we understand some basic things about how their minds work.[1]

What's Your Preference?

The theory of psychological types was based on Swiss psychologist Carl Jung's observation of the different ways people's minds work as they relate to the outer world. (His theory was further developed by Katharine Briggs and Isabel Myers over a period of nearly forty years.) Basically, the theory says that everyone was born with innate preferences in four main areas:[2]

1. Where you focus your attention and get your energy (extraversion or introversion)
2. What information you trust the most (senses or intuition)
3. How you make your decisions and judgments (logic or personal values)
4. How you like to structure your life (lifestyle)

As you use and develop your innate preferences, you develop a distinct way of relating to the world. The four preferences make up sixteen different combinations, or "types." Briggs and Myers researched and documented these combinations of traits and developed the *Myers-Briggs Type Indicator* (MBTI)™.*

Millions of people have taken the MBTI to find out their type; it is the most widely used personality indicator. The MBTI can only be administered by those who are trained and qualified to administer and interpret it. The best way to find out your "type" is to take the MBTI. (To find someone who gives it in your area, ask your pastor or a counseling center. Or contact the Association for Psychological Type (APT), 9140

*MBTI and *Myers-Briggs Type Indicator* are registered trademarks of Consulting Psychologists Press, Inc.

Ward Parkway, Kansas City, MO 64114, (816) 444–3500 for a list of people in your area who can administer the MBTI. Costs to take the MBTI vary, depending on the setting and purpose.)

I have found that an understanding of my preferences in each of the four categories has been an invaluable tool for helping me understand a key part of my design. It has also helped my self-esteem, as I learned to value the special qualities God designed into me (qualities that aren't always appreciated by the world at large).

Before we get into the specifics of this piece of your design, take a moment to pull out your notebook and do two exercises. These will put you in touch both with the way you wish your life would be and what it actually is. Then we'll use this information to find clues to your personal style.

Imagine the Perfect Week

Take a trip to fantasy land for a moment. Imagine you won a whole week to do whatever you want. How would you spend that week? I'm not talking about a vacation week, but how you would structure a perfect but "normal" week. How much time would you spend with whom? What would you do with all your hours? Spell it out. And be honest. If you love your work, include that and describe what you'd do. If you hate your work, write down how you would rather be spending your time (and don't be ashamed if part of that is being in the kitchen baking cookies, or spending part of each afternoon taking a nap).

Go into detail. Where would you be? With whom would you spend time? What would you do? How would you do it? How much time would you spend doing each thing you mention?

As an example, I've described for you my perfect week.

My Perfect Week

My perfect week would start with a Saturday. I would be free of all preplanned activities, ready for whatever this bright, sunny, spring day brings. For exercise, I would get up and take a walk by myself in the park near my house. I would note the orioles and finches, the waxwings, and perhaps even a killdeer or a heron. Then I'd go home and have a leisurely breakfast of whole-wheat waffles with my husband, Gene, and son, David.

After breakfast, David and I would go outside to work in my garden. He would play outside while I worked. Then we would go for a walk together, exploring whatever we could find. Then we'd have lunch. After lunch, my husband would take my son somewhere while I read a novel for the whole afternoon. Then I'd feed my son his supper, and my husband and I would go out for a leisurely dinner at our favorite restaurant, the Mill Race Inn. We'd come home and talk for awhile, then make love.

Sunday, I would go to church, and David would sit still and color his coloring book or look at a book quietly so I could actually worship. After church I would talk with my many friends there and participate in a stimulating Sunday school class. After a quick lunch at home, I would read the Sunday paper while our son napped. Then, when he woke up, we would go somewhere for a family outing. I'd have something made for supper; after supper would be stories and bath and bed for David. Then my husband and I would watch a video, or listen to a book on tape together.

Monday, Gene would go off to work, and David and I would spend the morning with friends (mine and his), preferably outdoors. We'd have a picnic lunch, then come home. He would take a nap, while I read a magazine or novel, or wrote in my journal. After he woke up, we'd maybe make something together. Then I'd make an interesting dinner, and we'd eat.

That night I might write a letter to a friend, or work on some writing of my own.

Tuesday, I would work, with David at a trusted sitter's. I would work on a book, either fiction or nonfiction. I would interview people and do book research as well as writing. At noon I would exercise and listen to my favorite radio show, then eat lunch with my husband. Then in the afternoon I'd finish my work for the day, maybe do a little housework (like laundry). (I'd be able to afford to hire a housecleaner in this fantasy!) Gene would make dinner that night, and we'd have a nice discussion at dinner, on which we would pick up and continue after David went to bed.

Wednesday, I would take David to story time at the library. Then we'd meet a friend for lunch. In the afternoon, we'd do some art work or some gardening. I would make dinner, we'd eat, and then I'd go back to the bookstore and spend the evening browsing at whatever struck my fancy.

Thursday, I would again write most of the day. In the afternoon I'd catch up with chores, maybe even decorate the house. After David goes to bed that night, I'd like to watch a mystery with Gene. Sex again.

Friday would be our "hang loose" day, to go wherever or do whatever came up. Some possibilities might be: visiting a children's museum, the zoo, a park; reading or making up stories; getting together with friends; participating in some Mom-and-kid class, and so on. In the evening we would join our church small group for dinner and Bible study.

Back to Reality

Now that we've imagined the ideal, let's get down to the real. How do you really spend your time in any given week? List all your activities.

To get your mind going, here's a list of possible activities:

Activity
Sleep
Cooking
Cleaning up kitchen
Cleaning house
Watching TV
Driving the car
Gardening/outdoor maintenance
Laundry
Reading
Writing letters/dealing with paperwork
Straightening house (making beds, clearing clutter)
Shopping
Fixing things
Getting ready for day
Making children's lunches
Helping with homework
Interacting with teachers/day care providers
Church activities
Meetings (church, volunteer organizations)
Talking on phone
Getting together with friends
Playing with children
Talking to husband
Planning meals/activities
Other

Now, beside each activity, rate the activity for how enjoyable it is for you and how much energy it either gives you or takes from you. Plus 5 means very enjoyable and energy-producing; 0 means you can take it or leave it; minus 5 means you hate it, and it's an energy-drainer.

Once you've done these two exercises, keep them before you as you go through the next part of our design discovery.

Where Do You Get Your Energy?

Exercise two gives you a quick overview of what gives you energy and what drains it. You might want to keep this chart in your notebook and add to it from time to time, as you try new things (or are forced to take on new things).

According to Jung, people tend to get their energy either from the outer world or the inner world of ideas. In type theory, Extraverts get their energy from people; Introverts glean energy from being able to turn inward for reflection.

Of course, all of us use both extraversion and introversion every day. However, we do our best work in either the outer or inner worlds and draw our energy from the outer or inner world. We have a preference for one or the other.

Looking over what you wrote down for the two exercises above, as well as thinking about how you prefer to operate in everyday life, might begin to give you a sense of which you prefer. The following paragraphs may also give you some sense of what the preferences look like in real life.

(Two things to note beforehand. First, there is no "better" way to be, though people may have made you feel one way is better than the other. Second, some of the things in each paragraph may apply to you.) It might be helpful to highlight or underline those descriptions that sound more like you and to cross out what definitely is not you.

Pam: Give Me Action

The first thing you notice about Pam's ideal week is that she is always on the go. She seems to thrive on stimulation from people, events, and things. Her ideal week includes taking in something new every day: going to a museum, shopping, going to a party, taking her children to the zoo, having people over for dinner, or working out at the health club. Everything she put down has to do with being with people or doing something active. Pam likes to know many people; nothing energizes her more than to meet someone new.

If you knew Pam, you would notice that she tends to think out loud. "I need people to bounce ideas off," she says. She shares information about herself freely. She is action-oriented; when a problem comes up, her immediate reaction is to *do something* about it. "Sometimes I act a little too quickly," she admits, "but I can't stand not trying to do something right away."

Pam's preference is for *Extraversion*.

Linda: Let Me Reflect

By contrast, Linda's ideal week is punctuated with significant "alone time" in which she can, in her words, "recollect myself." Though she planned her week to include people—having lunch with a friend, taking her children to the seashore, going out to dinner with her husband—her interactions were fewer and focused on the people she was already close to. "I don't really feel comfortable at things like parties where you have to meet a lot of new people. I'm never sure what to say to them." If Pam's byword is "breadth" in relationships, Linda's is "depth." "I prefer to get to know a few people really well."

Linda likes to keep a journal, in which she writes down her experiences and thoughts so that she can reflect on them. "Sometimes I'm not even sure what I think until I write it down," she says.

If you were to meet Linda, you would probably think of her as reserved. She doesn't show what's going on inside as readily as does Pam. It's not easy for her to "come up with an answer" right away; she wants to think about it first. When faced with a problem, Linda first mulls through the options inside her head before she feels comfortable sharing it with others.

Linda's preference is for *Introversion*.

Know Your Energy Source

With whom do you find yourself identifying most?

This may indicate your preference for Extraversion or Introversion. Remember, these terms are used here to specifically mean where you get your energy and tend to focus your attention. They are not an evaluation of your social skills. Many Introverts I know have very well-developed social skills. And not all Extraverts are "the life of the party." When in doubt, ask yourself whether you feel drained or energized by being in a large group of new people, for instance, at a party or conference.

You can also look to your "perfect week" scenario for clues. Note whether you wanted to be with people (Extravert), or whether you wanted to be alone (Introvert). When you were with people, was it with just those you know well and feel close to (Introvert), or were you meeting new people and having new experiences (Extravert)?

Getting a clear picture of your preference is crucial to making career-family decisions. Janet Penley, who has helped women apply type to their mothering, observes that we will do our best mothering when we are full of energy. Therefore, we need to know what fills our energy tank and what drains it.

Many mothers who work tell me that an outside job actually makes them a better mother. Other mothers say that their job just stresses them out. The difference between the first type of mother and the second is likely that she has a job that gives her energy. If she is an Introvert (like me), her job may give her the necessary time to work alone on her own projects; the time away from her children fills up her tank, so she comes back to the task of mothering with more energy. Or she may be an Extravert who finds staying at home all the time with little children to be too isolating. If she has a job that fills her need to be with adults and to have variety and challenge, she will return to mothering with her tank filled.

But if a mother is an Extravert, with a job that requires little interaction with other people, she is likely to come home feeling drained, with little left to give her children. Or if she is an Introvert with a "people" job, she will come home needing to recharge her batteries by being alone, yet faced with the (extraverted) tasks of mothering. So much depends on knowing your preference and working with it.

(By the way, Extraverts outnumber Introverts three to one in the general population. I grew up surrounded by Extraverts and always knew that I was different somehow. What a relief it was to me to understand that my "differentness" had to do with my preference for Introversion, and that I was "normal" after all!)

What Kind of Information Do You Attend To?

All of us have a preferred way of perceiving the world, of taking in information. Jung believed there were two equally valuable but opposite ways of taking in information.

Again, to get a sense of how this looks in real life, let's look at some examples.

Jean: Give Me the Facts

Jean is very in tune with the practicalities of life. In school, she said, she got very impatient with theory; she wanted to know of what use the theory was. She enjoys facts, remembers facts, trusts facts. (Playing *Trivial Pursuit* was on her list in her description of her ideal week.) She has no trouble tending to details and notices them naturally. She enjoys living in the present and is energized by sensory experiences.

Jean prefers to be with people who "say what they mean and mean what they say" and gets impatient when they "beat around the bush." When faced with a problem, Jean likes to look back on her own experience for insights on how to solve them, or to find out some standard way to solve it. She would rather "see the trees" than "see the forest."

Jean has a preference for *Sensing*.

Lauren: Give Me the Possibilities

Lauren is less concerned with facts than she is with possibilities. She trusts her intuition and "sixth sense" more than her five senses. She can hardly keep herself focused on the present because the future, with all its enticing possibilities, often intrudes.

Lauren thinks of herself as an "ideas person" who likes to focus on "the big picture" and see the patterns and meanings behind ideas. She enjoys poetry and fiction and all manner of figurative language. ("My cure for insomnia is to read a manual with charts and tables," she says with a laugh.) She enjoys finding new and novel ways of doing things, even simple things. She tends to "see the forest" rather than the "trees."

Lauren's preference is for *Intuition*.

Know Your Information Style

Not incidentally, our preference in this area affects how we communicate with others. Isabel Myers found that the difference between Sensing and Intuitive types marks the widest gulf between people. If you consistently find yourself shaking your head and wondering how on earth your husband or child can be the way they are, chances are they differ from you in this area. But can you see from the above descriptions how each preference has its own strengths and limitations? If we can begin to understand those, we can work toward appreciating not only ourselves but others as well.

How Do You Like to Make Your Decisions?

A third main area of preference is in how you make decisions. Here again, type theory uses terms a little differently than we do in everyday conversation. *Thinking types* base their judgments on impersonal, logical, objective data. *Feeling types* base judgments on personal, value-based, subjective criteria. Thinkers have feelings and Feelers can think! But the former tend to let their head rule their heart, while the latter let their heart rule their head.

Holly: Make It Logical

Holly feels most comfortable taking a logical, impersonal approach to decisions. It's not that she is unaware of feelings; these she factors in as part of the relevant data. For instance, when looking for a preschool for her child, she thoroughly researched the available options and made her decision. However, one of her children was clearly unhappy there. She carefully analyzed what might be the problem and realized that perhaps the program was too structured for her particular child. She then found an alternative that worked much better.

Holly governs her life by firmly held principles. She values justice and fairness. When someone has a problem, she believes she's showing love by helping to find ways to solve it. She has plenty of feelings but isn't very comfortable showing them. Her biggest struggle is that she easily sees what needs correction and is sometimes seen as too critical.

Holly's preference is *Thinking*.

Donna: Make It Harmonious

Donna takes a personal, values-oriented approach to her decisions and judgments. In making a decision about which preschool to choose for her child, for instance, she placed more weight on how happy the children seemed rather than on the reputation of the school.

Harmony is very important to Donna. She dislikes conflict and tries to smooth it over as quickly as possible when it happens. Her way of showing care is to let you know she understands; others experience her as warm and empathetic. Her biggest problem, she will say, is standing firm when she knows she should.

Donna's preference is for *Feeling*.

In the Minority

You may be interested in knowing that researchers in type theory have found that Thinking and Feeling are the only two preferences that seem to be linked to gender. Statistically, sixty percent of women and forty percent of men prefer Feeling, while forty percent of women and sixty percent of men prefer Thinking.[3] That's not a huge difference. But our culture overvalues Thinking and associates it with maleness. So women are generally brought up to be Feelers: relationship-oriented, warm, and personal.

If you, however, have a preference for Thinking, you may have felt out of the mainstream, a little odd. Yet there is a plus side to all this: Thinking women who were forced to develop their Feeling side will be more balanced than a man who has a preference for Thinking but never had to develop his Feeling side. If you find yourself on the line, ask yourself if your Feeling side is more of a result of natural preference or nurture.

Don't be afraid to be honest with yourself and to assess where your real preference lies and not what you feel is expected of you. As we'll see later, this preference is an important part of your design.

How Do You Like Your Outer World to Be Structured?

The final aspect of type, or personal style, has to do with how we like to structure our outer world. Again, type theory uses terms that are a little foreign to our everyday speech: Judging and Perceiving, but it's not difficult to understand the distinctions. Those with a preference for Judging—

Judgers—prefer to live life in a more structured way (making decisions), while Perceiving types—Perceivers—prefer a more spontaneous style (taking in information).

Beth: Give Me a List

Beth lives her life by her "to-do list." "I'd be lost without it," she admits with a laugh. She likes to plan and structure most aspects of her life and enjoys the sense of completion when she can check something off her list. She prefers closure and doesn't like to be "left up in the air" about a matter. She likes to work on one thing at a time, completing each thing before going on to the next.

Beth has a preference for *Judging*.

Marilyn: Go with the Flow

Marilyn feels hemmed in by too much structure or too strict a schedule. Although she does start out with a plan, she is quite willing to "go with the flow" if new information necessitates a change. She finds herself resisting closure; you never know, after all, how new information might change a decision. So when she and her husband needed to look for a used car, she wanted to take "just a little more time" in case "something better" came along. She prefers starting projects to finishing them and usually has more than one thing going on at any one time.

Marilyn's preference is for *Perceiving*.

A Difficult Preference to Discern

Janet Penley has found that the Judging/Perceiving preference is sometimes a difficult preference to decide if you're a parent, because having children stretches you to develop both aspects. Since you have responsibility for little people, you must be both organized *and* flexible. So as you think through which distinctions seem to fit you best, keep reminding yourself to assess what your *preference* is, not the way you actually function.

You might find it helpful to look at your description of your ideal week. Notice whether you tended to plan everything in detail or keep it the days open for "whatever may come along." Looking at my ideal week, I notice that I mention a "hang-loose day." This is one clue that my preference is Perceiving (which it is). However, a friend expressed astonishment at this preference of mine, because working from home as a freelance writer has forced me to function as a Judger much of the time. However, if I were truly a Judger, I would probably structure my weekends as closely as I structure my work days—and this I do not do!

Making Sense of Your Alphabet Tag

From these brief descriptions, some people with clear preferences are able to make a choice as to whether they prefer Extraversion (E) or Introversion (I), Sensing (S) or Intuition (N), Thinking (T) or Feeling (F), and Judging (J) or Perceiving (P). If you can't, that's all right. Take the MBTI, observe yourself in daily interactions, and/or talk over these things with a friend to see how others perceive you.

As you get a sense for your preference in each area, you will come up with a four-letter "alphabet tag" describing your type. There are sixteen possible combinations of the eight preferences, therefore sixteen different "types." Each type has unique characteristics that set it apart from the others. And each type is more than the sum of each of the letters; there is a dynamic interaction that takes place, so that changing even one letter may make that type very different from another type. If you would like to verify your type, I urge you to take the MBTI (Myers-Briggs Type Indicator). To find out more about your type if you already have taken the MBTI, I suggest you take a look at appendix A, or check out any of the books listed in the bibliography.

Some Words of Perspective

A few words of caution are in order as you think about type.

First, remember that *no one type is better than any other type.* No one type is more intelligent, more moral, more spiritual, or more emotionally balanced than another. If type is analogous to the colors of your design, ask yourself: Is the color green any better than the color red? Though our culture does tend to value some tendencies more than others, all of the types have strengths—and weaknesses. The best type for you to be is the one you *are.* Work on valuing that.

Second, understanding your type does not give you an excuse for wrong behavior. To say, "I can't expect myself to be organized because I'm a Perceiver (or Intuitive)" is wrong. I prefer both Intuition and Perception, and so organization and order are struggles, but that does not excuse me from trying to reach an acceptable level of both. Knowing, however, that this is a struggle for me helps me to be understanding of myself and empowers me to seek out the people and authors of books on organization who have that gift.

Which brings me to my third point: Type should be used to help us affirm our own and others' gifts, not to stereotype ourselves or others. I may be an INFP, which means I have many things in common with others who prefer Introversion, Intuition, Feeling, and Perceiving, but I express these preferences in my own way. And of course there's much more to me (and to you) than our personal style.

So let us use type to understand and embrace the beauty and value of our own design, to be more accepting of the differences of others (because "different" does not equal either inferior or superior), and to identify areas that need further growth in our own lives.

Now that we've looked at personal style or who you are, let's turn to what you like to do. These two elements, being and doing, are the foundation for designing a life you can love. Upon your knowledge of these two things you will build your own "house" that will incorporate your strengths and enable you to find a balance between family and work that is right for you.

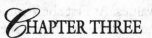

CHAPTER THREE

DISCOVER THE ENERGY OF YOUR DESIGN

*A*fter being a full-time homemaker and at-home mother of three children for fifteen years, Mershon Shrigley was ready to try something new. By this time her children were fifteen, ten, and four. Still feeling that her children needed her, she wanted something flexible, perhaps something she could do from home.

The question was, Where to start? Did she really need to go back to school to get a master's degree to prove she was "qualified"? After all, she had been out of the workforce for fifteen years. And though she had a B.A. in elementary education, she had never taught school: After college, while waiting to teach in the fall, an opportunity arose to work as a child-welfare social worker, and she jumped at the chance. She worked that job until her first child was born, then quit to be a full-time mom.

Mershon decided to take a career development course at a local community college to figure out her next step. Before investing a lot of time and money in another degree, she wanted to find out if she could build on the volunteer work she had done in her church and community.

Mershon took a good, hard look at her skills, interests,

experiences, and values. At first she assumed that her options were education and social work. But as she delved deeper into experiences that had given her the most satisfaction over the years, she came up again and again with three common threads: She enjoyed working with people of all ages, she enjoyed writing and creating tangible things (she had done newsletter editing and developed brochures), and she enjoyed teaching. She also realized she had good time-management skills, the ability to organize herself and motivate others, and a natural tendency to network with others.

Based on this knowledge, Mershon decided to start her own marketing-communications business. "It never would have occurred to me to do that if I hadn't taken the time to really look at my past experiences and evaluate where my skills were and what I enjoyed," Mershon says. She started her business on a part-time basis but within two years was up to full-time. Because she had established herself doing work she loved, her home-based business grew and prospered. Even when her husband ended their marriage of twenty-five years, her home-based business allowed her not only to support herself and her three children but to be available to give them substantial time and attention during and after the divorce.

Mershon is an example of someone who has designed a life she can love. But she didn't get there overnight. Let's look at the process she used to discover the skills upon which she built a new and successful career, one that she feels provides a nearly perfect balance between work and family life.

What Makes You Distinct

In the last chapter we looked at type, which gives you some handles on some general ways you approach your world. Now we want to get a bit more specific and help you see what your special, innate talents and attractions are.

There are certain things that make you unique, distinctive. You may not be aware of them; other people are usually more aware of our special strengths than we are. We tend to remember best the skills that were difficult to learn. But the fact that they were difficult to learn means that they did not draw on natural talent. With a skill based on natural talent, we can't remember ever learning it; somehow we just had the knack. We use these skills unconsciously and often overlook them until someone else points them out.

Once a friend said to me, "You really have a special way of using the phone to connect with people." I was amazed. To me I was just doing something that seemed so natural, something I assumed other people found easy too. It wasn't until I learned that many people feel uncomfortable on the phone that I realized that I seem to have a special knack for making other people open up over the phone. In fact, it has served me well in my work as well as my personal life; I have worked on many projects that require me to establish rapport over the telephone.

An important part of your design is made up of the special things that give energy and direction to your life. When you incorporate these into your life, you will live a life you can love. You will have the energy to do the things you must do that you don't enjoy much, because you will be drawing energy from things you love to do.

Look to Your Joy

How do you discover this energy within your design? Career experts like Bernard Haldane, Richard Bolles, and others have discovered that if you look at things you have done that you enjoyed and felt proud of, you will discover certain themes that run through your stories. That's because we tend to find ways to express our design, the essence of who we are, from a very early age. And we will continue to be drawn to activities that allow us to express our special strengths and gifts all through our lives. The sense of joy we get out of certain activities is what makes them "energized" for us; it's the clue that we are using our natural talents.[1]

Sometimes our earliest enjoyable activities provide the greatest clues to our natural talents, because as children we have the most freedom to engage in activities that naturally attract us. Novelist Ellen Gundersen Traylor remembers sitting up in a tree, writing poetry, when she was ten years old. Charlene Baumbich, an author and public speaker, used to stand with her friend on her front porch, making up ads and "selling soap on TV." Another time she agreed to give a speech between acts in a drama presentation at school, despite the fact that she had never taken any theater or drama classes. "I went from never being on the stage, to making up stories on the spot," she recalls. "I remember saying something, and everyone laughed. There was this wonderful sense of connection between me and the audience." Charlene had forgotten these experiences for decades. It was only now, as a public speaker—"something I never would have thought I would end up doing"—that she remembered these early experiences. The seeds of the adult's fruit are already present, even germinating, in the child.

Several years ago I saw a fascinating documentary called *Twenty-eight Up*. The filmmaker interviewed several people at ages seven, fourteen, twenty-one, and twenty-eight. It was fascinating to see how the experiences, attractions, and strengths of the child and adolescent matured into each adult. The last scene returned to the children at age seven, playing at the playground. Suddenly, with the knowledge of what each person became, you could see that what each person had become at twenty-eight was already hinted at in the activities of the child playing on the playground.

Step One: Remember Your Joys

The first step in discovering the "energy" of your design, then, is to look to the past for examples of you in action, doing something you enjoyed. Look for instances that stand out in your mind when you seemed to "flow" with what you were doing, when you felt particularly pleased with the outcome or the process. Jot these down in your notebook, simple one-line phrases of things you did at any time in your life, including childhood and adolescence, that you found enjoyable and satisfying. (For examples of satisfying activities, see the box.)

Sample Satisfying Activities

writing humorous poetry
learning to play volleyball
traveling to Ireland
composing birthday cards for friends and family
writing/editing for a newsletter
winning math contests
building and decorating a house for Barbie dolls
remodeling house with husband
participating in "May procession" in first grade
starting home-based business
learning from sister how to draw the spaces between things to make them realistic looking
conducting a survey on drug abuse in high schools
making my own multicolor crayon in kindergarten
volunteering at a local hospital as a teen
writing my own "novel" when I was ten
playing in a women's recreational soccer league and making friendships

---

Step Two: Find a Partner, Tell Your Stories

The second step is to find someone to listen as you tell your stories. It's easier for most of us (even Introverts) to tell our stories rather than write them out. Besides, it is easy to overlook our greatest strengths unless we have feedback from others. When you hear yourself describing these satisfying activities, you will begin to notice some recurring themes. Your partner will also notice some things you may have missed.

This step is fun for you and for your partner. It's simple. Sit down with your list of satisfying activities and a tape recorder. Your partner's job is simply to get you to tell your stories. Your job is to open up about the specifics of what you did. Your partner should ask:[2]

1. How did you begin this activity? What were you trying to accomplish?
2. Was there any kind of hurdle or restraint you faced? Describe it.
3. How did you go about doing this activity? (Make sure the person gets specific. You should be able to picture exactly how she went about accomplishing her task.)
4. What was the result of this activity—what did you accomplish?
5. What was satisfying to you about this activity? (Note that this is the most important question.)

To give you an example, here is the gist of a story I talked about when I went through this process.

Satisfying Activity: Tackled an English assignment in a particularly creative way and earned an A+

In my senior year of high school, I was in an Honors English class. My teacher gave me and two other of her top students an

---

assignment: to somehow prove that the protagonist of Camus' The Stranger. was innocent. I remember feeling blocked about it for days as the deadline approached, because I felt I had to do something really special with it after she assigned that.

I got a brainstorm some days before the deadline: I made up a trial scene in which the protagonist was being tried for murder. The narrator of the piece was the lawyer, who took the jury back to the scene of the crime, and step by step "proved" the defendant was innocent. I remember the feeling of exhilaration as I created this piece, which was really a piece of fiction but based on something objective. I think I wrote it during other classes, after school—just constantly, while the ideas flowed. I had a sense that this was a very creative approach, and I loved making up the scenes, putting in all the details that would make readers feel they were there. Also I liked the persuasive aspect of it; this narrator was trying to persuade people to his point of view, using evidence.

The teacher thought the paper was brilliant. She gave me an A+.

What was satisfying was the actual writing of the paper: the flash of insight, the sense of being carried along as I wrote, the discovery of what comes next as I wrote, the feeling of completion when I came to the end. I liked taking something from nothing, all the way to a finished product—planning how to do it, having control over each step. I also liked rising to my teacher's challenge.

As you tell your stories, you will probably feel a great deal of pleasure recounting what you did. Your partner should be noting those times when you seemed especially animated; you probably won't notice it because you'll be too involved in what you're saying!

Another thing your partner should note is any time you have repeated yourself as you tell your stories. For example, many of my satisfying activities involved writing, analyzing, learning, listening, imagining, creating. Other things that popped out in my stories were an attraction to ideas, a drive to maximize potential, a tendency to be in a pioneering situation. These things make up the core of my design.[3]

Step Three: Pinpoint Key Motifs

After you've told (and taped, for future reference) your stories, talk over your reactions with your partner. Which experience did you enjoy describing the most? What recurring themes did you notice? Jot down your ideas in your notebook.

Then ask your partner for her feedback. What struck her the most about your stories? What words and phrases did she note? Was there anything that struck her about your stories that you haven't mentioned? Add her notes to your list.

No doubt there were certain verbs that you and your partner noticed. These are your "energized skills," those things you do well with little effort. You should be able to pinpoint four to seven of these. (Going through the list on page 43 might help you.)

There will also be other motifs in your stories. Perhaps you find it particularly satisfying to work with animals, or children, or teenagers, or computers, or figures, or cloth. Perhaps it's a goal you consistently attempt to achieve—to maximize potential, or be the best, or manage others, or make things better. Or it might be a certain set of circumstances: Maybe you find that you particularly like to work on your own, or be part of a team, or be outdoors, or tackle a project from beginning to end.

You and your partner may find in your stories certain personal characteristics hinted at again and again. For instance, perhaps you were often in situations requiring "the courage to take risks," or "the ability to stick with a task despite obstacles," or "sensitivity to the feelings of others," or "the ability to concentrate despite distractions." Your partner is likely to notice these things quicker than you will. These characteristics are difficult to see in ourselves, but a trusted friend can easily spot and appreciate them.

After you and your partner have discussed some of the key themes in your stories, ask her to summarize what stood out to her as your particular talents. You should be able to pinpoint five to seven things that stand out from your stories. In your notebook, under "Key Motifs in My Design," write down from your stories those verbs and phrases that strike you as being most true of you.

These elements form the "outline" of your design, the basic pattern from which you will design a life you can love. Like the pattern from which you can make any number of pieces of clothing, depending on the fabric you choose and the variations you make in the basic pattern, so you can incorporate these elements into your life in various ways.

An Ongoing Process

Discovering your special strengths is an ongoing process. Listen to the tape again and see if you pick up any further themes. I also encourage you and your partner to continue to pay attention to things that provide joy and satisfaction. Continue to give each other feedback on what you see as strengths in each other. Most likely you will uncover more strengths and gifts as you start paying attention to your own satisfying experiences. As new ideas occur to you, jot them down in your notebook and get together to discuss them with your partner. Be open to giving and receiving feedback on the special gifts that you perceive in the other.

Now that you have at least the beginning picture of your design, let's start putting it to work. In the next chapter, we'll consider what we've learned so far in the light of your deepest values and come up with the purpose of your design—what you were put on this planet to do and be.

CHAPTER FOUR
A PURPOSE
YOU CAN LOVE

*S*ome years ago I bought a book, *The Type E* Woman: How to Overcome the Stress of Being *Everything to Everybody*, because the title caught my attention. *Boy, that's me*, I thought when I picked it up. Trying to be everything to everyone—a supportive wife, an outstanding employee, an attentive friend to several people, a dutiful daughter, a growing follower of Jesus Christ, an active church member.

I picked up the book today and again took the "Type E Stress Inventory." My scores had dropped significantly since my first assessment, years ago. I think I can say that, while I still battle with trying to be "everything to everybody," I have found a way to win that war. And it wasn't through learning the bag of psychological tricks that the author suggested, either.

I won the war when I began to fashion a sense of what I was put on this planet to do. Some call it a stated life purpose, others a personal mission statement; the Puritans called it a sense of calling. Once my "calling" or life purpose came into focus, I had a powerful tool for evaluating what I did, how I spent my time, what commitments I should and should not make.

The Benefits of Knowing Your Life Purpose

Taking the time to clarify my life purpose and write it down was one of the best things I ever did for myself. It gives my life a center from which all the spokes of my various roles and commitments radiate. When I'm feeling stressed from overcommitment, I go back to my life purpose and evaluate if there are any commitments I should drop because they are not in line with my life purpose. If there are, I can drop them without guilt or confusion. If not, I can readjust my thinking and my expectations. Often I find that I can find the motivation to pull me through a stressful time.

For example, I am now in a "crunch" period in which many things are happening at once. I have more work to do than I can possibly handle within the limits I have set for myself. (When you work for yourself, you have to be very strict about how much work you will or will not take on. I have said that I would not work more than three full days, no matter what, because for me it robs too much time from my family.) I have a deadline for this book and several other business pressures. New opportunities are opening up; should I go in this direction or that?

On top of that, people seem to be coming out of the walls with manuscripts on which they would like advice. It is spring, taxes are almost due, and I want to get out into the yard after a long winter. My son, David, is at an age where he is a lot of fun, and I long to go and play with him as much as possible. My husband is facing some important decisions, several people in my church are going through a crisis time, and one of my good friends and neighbors is about to have her second baby, and I said I'd help her in any way I could.

When faced with decisions, the needs of other people, change, or new opportunities, having a yardstick really helps. I have said yes to the opportunities that are in keeping with my life purpose and my values, no to those things that are not.

Doing this has meant that, for the next two months anyway, life will be stressful for me. But the stress is cut down significantly because I have a strong sense that I am doing what I'm supposed to be doing.

Having a sense of my unique life purpose also helps me overcome guilt. I can say no to being on the social committee at church, because it does not fit my design or my life purpose. In fact, saying yes would be wrong, on two counts. One, it would rob me of time I could be spending on something that is in line with my life purpose. (If I'm in committee meetings, I can't be with my family or able to write that column I'd promised for the church newsletter, say—two things that would be in keeping with my particular life purpose.) And two, it would deprive someone else, who would be perfect for the social committee, of using his or her gifts.

Finally, knowing my life purpose has helped me deal with change. Having a baby is a life-changing experience. Many, many women have reported that once they had children, they felt they "lost themselves" and their sense of who they are. I understand what they mean. Yet I have never felt I that I lost my sense of identity, though many things changed when I had David. I puzzled long and hard over why this was so, and I believe the answer is that I had already formulated my life purpose. This gave me a very grounded sense of who I am. Since my life purpose is general enough to include raising children, I just saw becoming a mother as one way of fulfilling my calling. As Stephen Covey says in *The Seven Habits of Highly Effective People*, if we have a changeless core inside of us—a changeless sense of who we are, what we are about and what we value—then we are able to accept change.

So what is a life purpose, and how do you go about developing one?

Start with Your Values

A life purpose or mission statement is grounded in your most deeply held values. Thus, developing your personal mission statement involves getting in touch with those values you hold most true and lasting.

As Richard Bolles reminds us in his inspiring little book, *How to Find Your Mission in Life*, our first two missions in life are shared by everyone. Yet, both are important and provide the context for the third mission, which is what I mean when I talk of a "life purpose."

The first mission we each share is summed up in Jesus' words: "Love the Lord your God with all your heart and with all your soul and with all your mind and with all your strength" (Mark 12:30). It is, as the Westminster Catechism says, "to glorify God, and enjoy him forever."

The second mission we each share is spelled out in the second greatest commandment: "Love your neighbor as yourself" (Mark 12:31). I like the way Richard Bolles interprets this: ". . . to do what you can moment by moment, day by day, step by step, to make this world a better place—following the leading and guidance of God's Spirit within you and around you."[1]

To discover the third part of our life purpose, we have to look again to our design, to the tools we have been given to accomplish the great calling to love the Lord with all we've got, and our neighbor as ourselves.

I believe that no one can accomplish those two tasks of loving God and neighbor in quite the same way Diane Eble can, and no one can accomplish those tasks in the same way you can. The world needs you to do your share. It's part of what it means to live out the prayer, "your kingdom come, your will be done on earth as it is in heaven" (Matthew 6:10).

How To Uncover Your Life Purpose

We discover this third part of our unique life purpose as we attempt to live out the first two parts. Clarifying your life purpose will take some time and reflection. Looking to the future can help to clarify our deepest personal values and sense of who and what we want to become and do.

So I propose another exercise, again using your imagination.

Start with the End

I recently had a dream in which I was cheerfully showing someone the basics of cooking. I was combining eggs and milk and flavorings and what-not. At one point, my student asked, "But what is it you're trying to make?" Embarrassed, I realized I didn't know.

It's ridiculous to try to cook without knowing what it is we're attempting to make. Yet some of us attempt to live our lives that way: We do this, we do that, with no sense of direction. A life purpose is the meaning of your particular life, so it's useful to start with the end product—what you hope your life will be in the end. So fast-forward in your mind to the end of your life. Imagine your funeral—or, if you prefer, your eighty-second birthday. Imagine a big party where everyone you've known through the years gets up and says something about you. What would you want to make sure you have accomplished in life before you die? What would you want others to say about you? When thinking about what "others" might say, be specific: What do you wish your husband would say about you? Your children? Colleagues? Friends? Other family members? People from your church, from your community?

Who would be at your party—lots of people whose lives you touched (Who? What specifically did you do to touch those lives?), or a few close family and friends who were spurred on to greatness because of you? Picture who would be there, hear in your mind's ear what they would say about you.

Write down your obituary. What phrases would you use to summarize who you were—your character? How would you summarize your accomplishments—what you did? In what specific ways has the world become a better place because you had walked through it?

See the box for a sample of how I have done this exercise.

Diane's Funeral and Obituary

At my funeral would be my family (husband, children, grandchildren, brothers, nieces and nephews, and so forth), my friends (from church, neighborhood, and work), fellow writers, and some strangers.

My husband would say that I always believed in him and helped him be all he could be. My children would say that I modeled what it was to love and be loved by the living God, that they saw a passion and joy in me for God that helped them also to know and love him. They would say that they learned from me what it means to enjoy life and to give it their all, and to cherish everything God created, from people to plants and animals. My brothers would say that I was kind, and a good friend, a support when they needed it.

My friends would say that I was there for them, that I had a unique way of listening and making them feel cared for and special. They would share some specific times when we laughed and cried together. People from my church would say that I was a friend to many. There would be a few people, friends of my children, who talk of having someone who would listen and care even when their own parents seemed too busy.

Others would be there—people I may not even recognize. Some are writers, who say they became writers because I helped them believe in themselves. Others would say that something I wrote helped them turn a corner in their lives, or made them

> *laugh or cry, or see God or themselves in a new way. Some would point to something I said or did, some way I worked with them or inspired them to be more than they thought they could ever be.*
>
> *My obituary would say: Diane Eble was someone who loved God and used whatever she had been given—material goods, knowledge, experience—to help herself and others live out their unique purposes. She was a writer who inspired and informed, and a wife, mother, and friend who cared. She loved her God, loved her family, loved her friends, loved her life, and tried not to waste a scrap of what she'd been given.*

⊗

Writing your obituary (or the glowing comments made at your eighty-second birthday party) is an example of what Stephen Covey calls "beginning with the end in mind." Too often we just start going, without first clarifying in our minds just where we want to go.

Many of the places I go habitually—grocery store, church, friends' houses—are in the same general direction. I get into my car, head out on Roosevelt Road, and on the way I call to mind exactly where I'm going. But to my embarrassment, I have occasionally headed down Roosevelt Road only to realize that this time I needed to go a different way! Sometimes I think we do that in life as well. We get into ruts and, as we speed down the road, rarely question whether we're really on the right road in the first place.

If writing your obituary or imagining your eighty-second birthday party doesn't appeal to you, try thinking through answers to the following questions:

- What kinds of needs, problems, and issues concern

you most deeply? Look at your whole life, not just work.

- If you could do what you really wanted, what would you do? If you didn't have to earn money, what would you do to feel useful?

When thinking through these questions, make sure your answers reflect your desires and not what you think others would expect of you. This is *your* life you're creating; don't let other people write the script of your life.

I urge you to take whatever time necessary to clarify what you hope to accomplish in your life. Take your time; a life purpose statement is something that evolves. Reflecting on these things is the first step.

Look to Your Design

The second step to clarifying your life purpose is to look back on what you've discovered about your design. It's especially helpful to identify your "energized outcome"—what it is you consistently tried to achieve in your Satisfying Activities. What is it that you are both passionate about achieving and uniquely gifted to accomplish?[2]

To put it another way, your life purpose should include what you need most to do and what the world most needs to have done.[3] A deep sense of meaning and purpose comes from having work that you love to do, and work that you know is contributing to more beauty, truth, love, or perfection to the world. As Frederick Buechner says, "The place God calls you to is the place where your deep gladness and the world's deep hunger meet."[4]

Three-part Purpose

I have found it helpful, in writing a life purpose, to think in terms of three parts. The first part takes into account the two things mentioned above: what you love to do, and what you want to achieve in the world. Thus, part one of my own life purpose is: "To help people discover God's purpose for their lives, so that they fulfill their potential and contribute toward making the world a better place."

Besides this summary statement that defines *what* you long to accomplish and the reason you want to accomplish it, add a "be" purpose and a "do" purpose.[5] Your "be" purpose includes the kind of person you want to become in order to accomplish your purpose. Your "do" purpose expresses the means for accomplishing your purpose.

My "be" purpose is: "To be someone who loves God and uses whatever he gives me (personal characteristics, knowledge, material goods) to help myself and others live out our unique purposes."

My "do" purpose is: "I believe my major means of accomplishing the above is through writing and personal relationships. I want to help people get in touch with their unique gifts through the books I write and the relationships I have with individuals."

This is the life purpose I wrote several years ago. Note that it is general enough to encompass a variety of roles and relationships: work, volunteer activities, family, friendships. And I can accomplish it through a variety of means: writing, speaking, mothering, mentoring, consulting.

In fact, your life-purpose statement should flow out of key elements of your design: the energized abilities, personal qualities, and other key motifs you identified in the last chapter. My life purpose encompasses my key energized abilities of communicating and building relationships, and my "energized outcome" (what I try to do in my Satisfying Activities), which is to help others maximize their potential.

My life purpose has not changed since I wrote it. What has changed is the number of opportunities for fulfilling it. I became a mother—certainly an opportunity for fulfilling this particular life purpose. New opportunities for speaking, consulting, and mentoring have opened up. It is almost as if, once I wrote down my mission statement, opportunities materialized for fulfilling it. I believe what's really happened, however, is that because I have become focused on my particular mission, I have both opened myself up to opportunities for fulfilling it and have cleared away obstacles that would blind me to the opportunities that are there.

You may choose a different way to write up your life purpose statement. Some people prefer to state their life purpose as a sort of "credo," a short list of their most important values and goals. For instance, one ENFP woman wrote up her mission statement thus:

1. To love God with heart, soul, and mind.
2. To love myself and others in a healthy way.
3. To be honest with myself and others.
4. To maintain balance in my life.
5. To use my talents for creativity and organization, and my ability to form strong relationships, to create a better world.
6. To take care of the resources God has given to me (body, mind, soul, nature).
7. To enjoy life and live it to the fullest and help others do the same.

This person still includes a "what" (loving, using talents, taking care of resources, enjoying life, and so on) and a "why" that are based on her energized outcome and her spiritual gifts of serving and perceiving (create a better world, help others do the same). She draws upon her key energized abilities (creativity, building relationships, and organization).

If you prefer to list your key values and goals in this format, go right ahead. No doubt how you choose to state your life purpose will also reflect your individual style! Just make sure it can be accomplished in both personal and professional settings. Your identity will be based on your ability to fulfill your mission in any setting.

Making It Personal

Now it's time to start to formulate your own personal mission statement. Take some time to skim the summary of your design from the end of chapter 3. If you haven't already done the suggested exercises (imagining the end of your life, writing your obituary, or answering the two questions starting on page 55), do so now. Reflecting on these elements, answer the question, "What is it that I love to do, feel uniquely gifted to do, that the world needs done?" Summarize your answer. Then write down the kind of person you want to become in order to achieve this purpose, and the means you want to use to accomplish your purpose.

Keep your life-purpose statement handy to review every day. It will prove a very useful compass for making the kinds of decisions we will look at in part 2 as we look at various options for making your design work in the real world of babies and active, growing children, and careers.

Life Purpose Statement

I believe I was put on this earth to _____ so that _____.
I want to become the kind of person who _____.
I want to accomplish my life purpose by _____.

PART TWO

DESIGNING YOUR LIFE

CHAPTER FIVE

DESIGNING YOUR OWN MOTHERING STYLE

*M*y friend Heather and I are very different mothers. Heather is a single mom with two children—Karl, eleven, and Karen, nine. She is very good at structuring activities for her kids. She is also able to take an objective approach to problems her kids are having. In fact, I often marvel at her ability to be objective. When her daughter won't eat and her son misbehaves in school, she adopts a very logical, objective, step-by-step approach to dealing with those problems.

A few years ago, when the kids were younger, I remember her telling me she was feeling stressed every morning because the kids were not getting up on time. She had to be at work at a certain time, and the kids needed to dress and eat and be on their way to day care. In keeping with her personal style, she was able to step back and analyze exactly what the problems were and what steps she could take to alleviate them. She bought each child an alarm clock and showed them how to set it. She expected them to set their clothes out and set the table for breakfast the night before. And if they dawdled when getting dressed, they might just miss their breakfast. "They'll be hungry, but then they'll learn," she said to me matter-of-factly.

Heather clearly has no problem using what Dr. Kevin Leman calls "reality discipline." Letting the kids experience the logical consequences of their actions makes eminent sense to Heather. Very disciplined and responsible herself, she expects her children to also learn self-discipline and responsibility. These are some of her strengths.

I am quite different. When my child has a problem, I immediately try to understand it. I want to solve the problem by *understanding* my child and the problem and usually offer empathy before I offer any kind of objective solution.

However, sometimes a more logical, objective approach is better. I believe in "reality discipline," but it's not easy for me to implement. And sometimes my son sends signals that I am too much in his face. I struggle to give him the space he needs to grow as an independent, separate individual. There are many times I know that I (and David) could benefit from some of Heather's ability to step back and find step-by-step, objective solutions!

Developing your own style of mothering, based on your design, can free you from the trap of comparing yourself to other moms. It will help you capitalize on your strengths and understand your struggles. I also hope it will allow you to give yourself permission to see that your own legitimate needs are met and to find ways to balance your mothering style with some other approaches.

Janet Penley is a mom who has developed a seminar called M.O.M.S.™ (Mothers Of Many Styles). As she says, good mothers come in many styles. Knowing your style and building on your strengths will help you become comfortable with this aspect of your life, which will, in turn, as we shall see, affect how you feel about juggling other areas of your life as well.

Becoming the Best Mom *You* Can Be

I start with applying your design to your mothering rather than to the career decisions because I believe the career should always be in service to our parenting, not vice versa. Mothering demands the best of who we are as we invest in the next generation.

Understanding what mothering involves and comparing that to your own design will help you to develop your own mothering style. It will also, I hope, enable you to pinpoint areas of your life that are drained by the demands of mothering, so that you can set more realistic standards for yourself in those areas. Finally, it will help you to make wise decisions about how to express key elements of your design that are not expressed in mothering.

What Mothering Involves

In your notebook, write up a job description of a mother. Include both what a mother *does* and what a mother *is*.

In terms of doing, parenting probably requires more skills than any other job we're called on to do. In his book, *What Color Is Your Parachute?*, Richard Bolles lists 250 possible skills one could use in life (see below). As I studied that list, I counted 173 skills that parenting requires at one time or another!

List of 250 Skills As Verbs[1]

achieving	analyzing	assessing
acting	anticipating	attaining
adapting	arbitrating	auditing
addressing	arranging	budgeting
administering	ascertaining	building
advising	assembling	calculating

charting	dramatizing	influencing
checking	drawing	informing
classifying	driving	initiating
coaching	editing	innovating
collecting	eliminating	inspecting
communicating	empathizing	inspiring
compiling	enforcing	installing
completing	establishing	instituting
composing	estimating	instructing
computing	evaluating	integrating
conceptualizing	examining	interpreting
conducting	expanding	interviewing
conserving	experimenting	intuiting
consolidating	explaining	inventing
constructing	expressing	inventorying
controlling	extracting	investigating
coordinating	filing	judging
coping	financing	keeping
counseling	fixing	leading
creating	following	learning
deciding	formulating	lecturing
defining	founding	lifting
delivering	gathering	listening
designing	generating	logging
detailing	getting	maintaining
detecting	giving	making
determining	guiding	managing
developing	handling	manipulating
devising	having	mediating
diagnosing	responsibility	meeting
digging	heading	memorizing
directing	helping	mentoring
disciplining	hypothesizing	modeling
discovering	identifying	monitoring
dispensing	illustrating	motivating
displaying	imagining	navigating
disproving	implementing	negotiating
dissecting	improving	nurturing
distributing	improvising	observing
diverting	increasing	obtaining

offering	recording	supplying
operating	recruiting	symbolizing
ordering	reducing	synergizing
organizing	referring	synthesizing
originating	rehabilitating	systematizing
overseeing	relating	taking
painting	remembering	taking instructions
perceiving	rendering	talking
performing	repairing	teaching
persuading	reporting	team-building
photographing	representing	telling
piloting	researching	tending
planning	resolving	testing and
playing	responding	proving
predicting	restoring	training
preparing	retrieving	transcribing
prescribing	reviewing	translating
presenting	risking	traveling
printing	scheduling	treating
problem solving	selecting	trouble-shooting
processing	selling	tutoring
producing	sensing	typing
programming	separating	umpiring
projecting	serving	understanding
promoting	setting	understudying
proof-reading	setting-up	undertaking
protecting	sewing	unifying
providing	shaping	uniting
publicizing	sharing	upgrading
purchasing	showing	using
questioning	singing	utilizing
raising	sketching	verbalizing
reading	solving	washing
realizing	sorting	weighing
reasoning	speaking	winning
receiving	studying	working
recommending	summarizing	writing
reconciling	supervising	

Used by permission of Richard Bolles.

Look at Bolles's list and think about how many you use every day in your parenting. How many of them show up on your list of energized abilities from chapter 3? Is there any overlap at all?

If you look at mothering as a job, requiring specific skills, you can evaluate whether your energized abilities and parenting skills match.

Matching Your Mothering to Your Skills

Those women who find they can major on at least one or two of their energized abilities in their mothering will likely feel more fulfilled than women who find less of a match. The positive side of the fact that parenting requires so many skills is that we will most likely find ways to use our natural talents in our mothering.

For instance, I am energized when I can create, discover, imagine, learn, listen, nurture, and write. I am designing my own mothering style to major in these areas. I create songs, projects, and other fun things to do. We often go places as a family where we can discover and learn new things. I find it easy to listen to my son and to nurture his growing abilities. And I write things down in a family journal that I hope to give my son someday. I derive great joy and satisfaction in using these skills in my mothering.

I also use these same energized skills to nurture myself. I create new recipes and household systems. I listen often to the radio, or read, to feed my need to learn and discover. I garden and snuggle up to my cats to express my nurturing instincts. And I write, to know what I'm thinking and feeling.

Look through your list of energized abilities that you identified in chapter 3. In what ways can you use those in your parenting? In what ways can you use them to nurture yourself?

Now look at the other elements of your design that you isolated. Are there self-management skills you can build on? If you're a self-starter who has always dreamed of starting your own business, you may well have what it takes. If you're competitive, you might want to make sure you include sports of some kind into your life. If you can concentrate well despite distractions, you may be able to get work done at home even with children around.

You'll also want to take into account other aspects of your design that you discovered, such as a strong preference for a particular subject matter, specific results you try to achieve, or certain roles or circumstances you find particularly energizing. Any of these things that you noted running through your Satisfying Activities can be incorporated into your own mothering style. Certainly your preferred subject matter and energizing outcome—what it is you consistently tried to accomplish in your Satisfying Activities—have a direct relationship to your mothering. But the most important aspect of your design to take into account in developing your mothering approach is personal style.

Let's look at some ways you can match some of these key elements of your design to the demands of parenting.

Preferred Subject Matter

Obviously, moms who prefer to work with people will find mothering easier than those motivated to work with things or information. However, moms who do prefer things or information can incorporate these into their parenting.

For instance, Sandy likes to sew. Above everything else, she prefers to work with her hands. When her children were young, she started her own business, sewing bibs. She loves to get down on the floor and play with blocks or Legos with her children. As her children got older, she devoted more time to her business. She also began to teach her daughter how to sew. Sewing and doing things with her hands became her refuge, her livelihood, part of her identity, and a way to spend time playing with and teaching her children.

My preferred subject matter is information. I read about child development so I know what to expect at each stage. I enjoy learning new things and helping my child to learn new things. I enjoy swapping information about children and child-raising with my husband and my friends.

Energizing Outcomes

You may have noticed in your Satisfying Activities that there was a particular result you often tried to achieve. For me, it's to maximize potential. For others it might be to serve, to gain recognition, to excel, to be distinctive, to improve something or someone—the possibilities are many. Some outcomes lend themselves more readily to parenting than others. If you're energized when you can serve, shape and influence, or meet needs, parenthood will probably be satisfying. If you're motivated to acquire, to be in charge, to improve or make better, to name a few possibilities, you may feel more frustrated with parenting. However, understanding this part of your design can help you to find appropriate ways to express your inclination.

Let's suppose, for instance, that you are a mother of three young children, and your Satisfying Activities point to a strong need to gain recognition or attention. You will probably find it difficult to be at home with young children, since this occupation is generally not recognized by our society as a worthwhile activity. However, you can gain the recognition you crave through volunteer work or a job. Trying to get this need met by your children (or even your husband) is likely to lead to frustration.

Each "energizing outcome" has a positive and negative side. I can find many positive ways of maximizing my energizing outcome, from devising a creative use for something rather than tossing it, to being aware of my child's emerging personality and looking for ways to help him be all he can be. The pitfall of my energizing outcome is that I have a very low tolerance for waste. I get very frustrated when I see someone in my family wasting money, or time, or some other resource. I have to remind myself that this is part of *my* design, not theirs, and that I can't expect them to be motivated in the same way I am.

What is your energizing outcome? What ways can you use it positively in your parenting? What problems have you experienced in expressing this part of your design? Write your answers in your notebook, under a section titled "My Design for Mothering."

Personal Style

Parenting will stretch you, no matter what you have found your personal style to be. Just as it calls on almost every skill imaginable, so it requires you to use every possible preference in the personality-type scenario. Mothering calls upon the ability to constantly relate to family members (Extraversion), and the ability to call upon inner wisdom for making decisions (Introversion). We need to develop our Sensing to keep track of small children and their activities (when they're too noisy—signifying a squabble—or too quiet, signifying another sort of mischief). We depend on our Intuition to understand our children, come up with better ways to foster their growth, and be alert to possible dangers. We must use Feeling to create harmony in the home and teach our kids empathy; and Thinking to analyze and organize, and think through and teach by logical consequences of actions. Finally, mothering requires both constantly planning ahead (Judging), and constantly adapting to changes in our well-laid plans (Perceiving).

If parenting calls upon such diverse strengths, you will

bring both strengths and struggles to mothering. Knowing what these are will help you both pat yourself on the back for what you're doing right and give yourself some leeway in the areas in which you struggle.

Janet Penley has studied type theory in depth and has applied it to mothering styles. Penley says, "Kids don't need perfect moms, but moms who have come to terms with their strengths and weaknesses." Most of us have some image of the "perfect mom." My image is of someone who is always available, always giving, always knows what to say and do, never loses her temper with her kids, is able to keep her house organized and get her children to all their activities on time. She does all this with a smile and blissful joy, of course.

The reality is that I have certain strengths and weaknesses that both I and my children will have to contend with. But if I believe God is sovereign, I will trust that he not only gave me my children, but he gave them me as their mother. My very strengths and weaknesses are part of what he will use to shape them into the people they are meant to be.

Following are some of the strengths and struggles of each preference that Penley has identified, and some tips she offers for nurturing yourself so that you can be the best mom you can be.[2]

Extravert

Mothering Strengths: A strength of the Extraverted mom is her ability to get out and help her children experience the world. Extraverted Fiona, a mom with four children under the age of six, says she likes taking her kids out, whether to the grocery store or to the zoo. Not surprisingly, there are always neighborhood kids in her house. "The more the merrier" seems to be her motto. The Extraverted mom thrives at a busy pace and can inspire others with her prodigious energy and enthusiasm.

Struggles: An Extraverted mom will find it difficult to be isolated at home with babies and preschoolers, no matter how strongly she feels it is the right thing to do. Because she's tuned in to others, she may find it difficult to tune out the expectations of society and of others. Fiona loved staying home with her children but found it very difficult to deal with her mother's comments about how she was "wasting her mind" by staying home, and with society's general lack of respect for her decision to be a full-time mother.

Tips: For the Extraverted mom, working within her personal style means having variety, action, and people. She will enjoy being on the go, involved in several activities. Taking time away from the children to be with friends will feed her Extraversion and replenish her in a way that being with children cannot.

Yet, even Extraverted moms may feel over-extraverted by the demands of caring for an active family (and maybe combining that with a career). They, too, need some quiet time to recollect their thoughts, to tune in to God and their own inner wisdom.

Introvert

Mothering Strengths: The Introverted mom gravitates toward spending time observing and reflecting about each of her children; she respects and fosters their individuality and wants to know them in depth. She tends to provide a quiet and calming presence (even though inside she may feel anything but calm!).

Struggles: Mothering is largely an outwardly oriented task. An Introverted mom will find it draining to constantly be turned outward to children and all the things that have to be done. One mother of two preschoolers described her day: "From the time I get up in the morning until I get them tucked in at night, my entire day is focused on the boys. It's often nine o'clock in the evening before I have any time to myself, and by then I'm so exhausted I just want to go to bed and get some sleep."[3] Such a scenario would exhaust even an Extravert but will be so draining for an Introvert that she would probably find herself reaching her limits well before nine o'clock, and either lashing out from exhaustion or otherwise showing stress.

Tips: For the Introverted mom, "alone time" is not a luxury but a necessity, for this is her source of energy. She needs at least a half hour every day for solitude. This may call for creativity. Some moms hire a teenager to watch the children in the afternoons, while they pursue some solitary activities. Others train their children not to disturb them during a certain period every day.

The Introverted mom might also look for ways to meet her children's need for external stimulation that don't involve her. Play groups, mom's morning out, preschool, music, art or other classes, recreational centers that offer child care, can all give both her and her child what is needed.

Sensing

Mothering Strengths: Moms who prefer Sensing like to focus on "what is"—the facts. They gravitate toward meeting the practical needs of their children, making sure they have enough to eat, that they are clean, well-rested, that their homework is done, that they have a way to get to their activities, and so on. They are good at helping their children get along in the real world and at keeping life simple and grounded in the here-and-now.

Struggles: A Sensing mom may find it hard to tune in to a child's fantasy life. She may have trouble seeing that the hooded towel her preschooler is wearing is a "Batman cape." To her it just looks like a towel.

A Sensor may also find it harder to see all the possibilities in difficult or complicated situations.

Tips: For Sensing moms, rejuvenation comes from feeding the senses. Pull out the china and eat a late candlelight meal with your husband once in a while. Or sit down just to listen to some beautiful music. Or take a bubble bath.

Don't worry about joining your children's fantasy play. They will find other avenues that will help stimulate their imagination.

If you find it hard to see possibilities, find an Intuitive to "brainstorm with." One Sensing friend of mine felt overwhelmed by her son's problem with Attention Deficit Disorder. She benefited by sitting down with an Intuitive mom to brainstorm ways of dealing with the situation, and did end up getting help. Or sit down with your children and, in a playful way, consider new possibilities: ten fun things you might do on your next vacation; twenty different things to do with soap bubbles; eight ways to decorate your child's birthday cake.

Intuitive

Mothering Strengths: Intuitive moms value creativity and imagination, and so excel in encouraging it in all its forms: making up games or songs, pretending, making things, attending cultural and artistic events. They are good at pointing out possibilities and options, and offering children choices. They look for and encourage the unique potential in each child and are usually comfortable with a child who acts or thinks differently from them.

Struggles: Intuitive Moms may be worn out by the constant attention they must pay to the myriad details of life. They must not only meet their children's everyday needs but also know their whereabouts and activities at every moment. Because she tends to be idealistic, an Intuitive is often disappointed when life and her children fall short of the ideal. Always attuned to possibilities, she may find it hard to simply take pleasure in the moment—and to keep things simple.

Tips: Intuitives are exhilarated by the opportunity to entertain new ideas, perspectives, and dreams. Going to a parenting class, reading parenting books, and talking over new ideas with husband or friends, all will feed their strength and contribute to their mothering skills. Listening to talk radio is another possible way to connect with the world and to stimulate ideas without having to leave the house.

Intuitives may need to consciously take time to live in the moment—to stop to notice and enjoy what's coming in through the senses. Another way to develop Sensing is through play—by participating in children's art projects, for instance, or playing board games with them.

Thinking

Mothering Strengths: Moms with a preference for Thinking (using logic and impersonal analysis) are good at encouraging their children to think and do for themselves, promoting self-reliance and self-sufficiency. They find it easy to teach and modify behavior through the use of logical consequences and cause and effect. Thinking moms value and affirm their child's achievements, and foster competency and a can-do attitude.

Struggles: A Thinking mom may find it hard to tune in to and be patient with feelings, especially when they seem irrational, are "going nowhere," or have no basis in reality. A Thinking mom may find it difficult to accept a child as he or she is. Because it's easy for her to spot flaws and natural to give honest feedback, she may come across as critical if she doesn't make sure she also offers appreciation and praise.

Tips: A Thinking mom has a strong need for validation of her competence. Because this culture does not value mothering consistently, her mothering role may be a source of frustration.

She may need to remind herself that she doesn't need to prove herself in order to be loved.

A Thinking mom who finds it uncomfortable to deal with feelings may need to remind herself that sometimes feelings just need to be; not everything can be "fixed" by logical problem-solving. Also, when making decisions, she can take the view that feelings are part of the facts of the situation, and just as important as facts and logic.

Feeling

Mothering Strengths: Feeling moms find it quite natural to give their children the physical and emotional closeness they need to feel loved, special, and secure. They are attuned to feelings and responsive to needs. They naturally look for what's good in a child, accepting and affirming him or her.

Struggles: Because she's so in tune with her children's needs, a Feeling mom may find it difficult to keep her emotions separate from her children's problems. For instance, she may be devastated when her child is rejected by peers. Or she can be manipulated by her child's anger or sweet talk. She may also neglect identifying and meeting her own needs; she feels guilty when her attention has not been totally on her children.

Tips: To take care of herself, a Feeling mom needs to take a break from caring for other people's needs, and put her own needs first at times. A Feeling mom may have to remind herself again and again that getting her legitimate needs met is *good* for her children. Martyrs only instill guilt and resentment in their children. A mother who takes her own needs into account gives a clear signal that she, too, is important and that instills respect.

Judging

Mothering Strengths: The mother who prefers a Judging style excels at organizing and planning day-to-day living so that her children don't miss out. She's not caught unaware when it comes to permission slips, lunch money, snack for snack day, camp physicals, and the like. She keeps daily routines on an even keel, and makes a smooth-running, orderly household a priority. Through her words and her actions, she teaches children how to get a lot done through organization, planning, discipline, focus, and follow-through. She values time management and encourages children to respect and use their time wisely.

Struggles: Unfortunately for Judgers who find satisfaction in completing tasks, motherhood is never completed. It is an ongoing process, full of the unexpected and last-minute changes. Thus, frustration over "never getting things done" is a constant struggle. She may find it difficult to relax and have fun when there are still things that need to be done.

Another struggle has to do with the mess, noise, and chaos that children bring to a home. One way to deal with this is to claim one room or area of the house as your own— a place where you can keep things your way.

Tips: Letting go of the "shoulds" and of doing things the "right" way may be a difficult but worthwhile endeavor for a Judging mom. She would benefit from making it a priority to take time for fun, actually scheduling it in on her "to do" list! She can find new ways to have fun with her children. If she has trouble thinking of possibilities, she can think back to what she enjoyed when she was their age.

When feeling frustrated about the inability to control what her children do, a Judging mom can concentrate on organizing and finishing some project or task that is under her control—doing the laundry, cleaning out a drawer, making phone calls for the church picnic.

Perceiving

Mothering Strengths: The Perceiving mom is gifted at being flexible and adaptable to the flow of life with children.

She is tolerant and able to let her children be themselves without pushing or trying to shape them. She's not as bothered by interruptions and can be responsive to her child's needs of the moment.

Struggles: There is a downside to being tolerant of chaos: Household tasks may get away from you. One Perceiving mom said, "I never have trouble having fun with the kids. But suddenly it's five o'clock, the house is a mess, my husband comes home, and I haven't given a thought to dinner." Living with everyday routines and sameness is draining for a Perceiver.

A Perceiving mom may also have trouble keeping her children on task and on time—getting them to bed at a decent hour, getting them out the door in the morning for school. She may find it stressful to juggle everyone's schedule and to stay focused on finishing a task. She may find herself taking on way too much.

Tips: A Perceiving mom does best when she can function with spontaneity; therefore, freedom from too tight a schedule will energize her. Janet Penley recommends allowing at least one slow, unscheduled morning on the weekend to "hang out" and recover from the busy week. Because time is more fluid for the Perceiver, when trying to get things done it's often helpful to list one to three things that *must* get done, and stay flexible to handle whatever else the day may bring. Also, rather than holding herself to too many rules, set a few basic intents. I like what one local preschool set for rules: "Be kind, be careful, be clean." Sticking to the basics helps a Perceiver from feeling boxed in.

Accept Your Style—and Theirs

I've often puzzled over why two people could have grown up in the same family, and one found it dysfunctional and the other thought it was great. I've since come to the conclusion that so much depends on the "fit" between child and parent—and much of that "fit" has to do with a good match between parent and child. Parents who value each child for who he or she is, even if the child is very different from them, will be able to offer the acceptance and affirmation the child needs to grow up into his or her full potential. Sadly, too often when there are personality differences between parent and child, the parent fears there is something wrong with the child. Parents may misunderstand the child. They may find it hard to offer the kind of approval the child needs, and the child's self-esteem begins to suffer.

Some examples of mismatch would be the Extraverted mom who tells her Introverted daughter she "has no personality" because she is not outgoing; the Introvert who can't understand why her child "always needs to be with friends"; the Sensor who spanks her Intuitive daughter for "lying" when she's just exercising her imagination; the Intuitive who thinks her child is "slow" because she needs to have things spelled out step by step; the Thinker who tells her son he's "too sensitive"; the Feeler who tells her daughter she's "not affectionate enough"; the Judger who doesn't understand her child's "lack of responsibility"; and the Perceiver who doesn't understand why her daughter has to have things "just so."

No doubt this chapter has not only helped you understand your own strengths, struggles, and needs but also some of the reasons you may clash with your husband or children. Learning to understand and appreciate both differences and similarities in personal style will enable you to be a better mother.

Generally, you will understand and communicate better with a child or spouse whose style is similar to your own. However, you will also see your own weaknesses magnified in them.

If a child is very different from you, it will take an extra effort to understand and communicate with him or her. Take the time to understand and appreciate your children's unique styles. Sit back and observe; take the attitude that you have something to learn from your child as well as to teach him or her. Do not attempt to treat each of your children in the same way; they are each different people with different needs. Try to discover what those needs are and act accordingly.

Learn to speak your child's "language." For instance, with a Sensor, focus your communication on facts and specific, concrete information. Intuitives prefer enthusiastic, colorful, imaginative language. Thinkers want brief, concise statements that point out the reasons why. Feelers respond best when empathy and personal interest is expressed.

Realize, too, that our culture, and the school system, is biased toward certain preferences. The culture overvalues Extraversion, Sensing, Thinking (except when it comes to girls, who are socialized toward Feeling), and Judging. If you, or your children, have the opposite preferences, you will be "swimming upstream" in some ways. Affirm your own or your children's preferences for Introversion, Intuition, Thinking-Feeling, and Perceiving.

No matter what your preferences are, you can use them to inform and enrich your mothering. Forget what your neighbor or your sister is doing; concentrate on what God has gifted you to do, and do it the best you can!

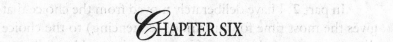

CHAPTER SIX
SEQUENCING: DESIGNS FOR THE SEASONS OF LIFE

So far in this book we have concentrated on you—your gifts, your abilities, your motivations, your personal style. Knowing these elements of your design is critical; however, they are not the sole things to consider when you are trying to design a life you can love. Your circumstances present a big factor to weigh when seeking options for applying your design to the real world. You have a husband, perhaps, or you're single or widowed or divorced. You have children, or are considering having children, or have decided you don't want children. Your finances impose certain limitations or freedoms. You or a member of your family may have a special need that also shapes your choices.

To make a good decision about the best combination of work, personal life, and family for you, we need to first consider the facts: your design, your circumstances, available resources, and the needs of each family member. Then we will look at the possibilities and options, based on these givens. Next, it's wise to consider the advantages, tradeoffs, and likely consequences of each option. Finally, you will want to weigh the desirability of each option in human terms—how it affects you and your family on a personal level.[1]

In part 2, I have deliberately moved from the choice that gives the most time for nurturing (sequencing) to the choice that concentrates the most effort on work (working full-time outside the home). If God has given us two responsibilities, to nurture and to work, common sense tells us that for women with children, there will be times when one or the other responsibility will take priority. At certain times one task will be in the foreground, the other in the background of the picture of our life. Then, as family circumstances change, the picture shifts.

The Seasons of a Woman's Life

Several years ago, before I even had children, I saw and bought a book called *Sequencing: Having It All But Not All At Once*. The author, Arlene Rossen Cardozo, pointed out that raising children and building a career are each full-time tasks. I was in the midst of building a career myself at the time and knew it did indeed take up most of my time and energy. I couldn't imagine adding a child to the mix; I knew that something would have to give.

Cardozo's book made me realize that indeed, there is a way to "have it all but not all at once." The key was in what she calls *sequencing:* First, get an education and gain some career experience; then leave full-time work during the years when children are young; and then, as the children grow, find new ways to incorporate professional activities back into your life in such a way that mothering and profession do not conflict.

In reflecting on the unique challenges women face in planning their career and life, I have found it helpful to think in terms of seasons of life. Each season has its own special opportunities and characteristics. As we look for ways to express our design in each of these special seasons, I believe we will find a satisfaction that is very special to womanhood.

Seasons Without Children

Typically, the first season of a woman's life is the season in school. We get our education, we get trained. The majority of us are single during this season of training. Afterward, we may get started in a career. Some of us also get married.

The season of singleness, whether it lasts for a short time or for all of a woman's life, can be a very special time. In a culture that pushes people to pair up, it's easy to lose sight of the advantages of singleness. Singles have freedoms any married woman with children covets: the freedom to travel, to progress in your career, to go out when you feel like it, to concentrate on your own spiritual and personal growth. You can express your design wholeheartedly, without having to compromise endlessly because of the needs of other people. You are free also to serve in ways that married women with children often can't.

The apostle Paul, who was apparently single, thought it such an advantage that he said he wished everyone could be like him. To him, singleness wasn't second best; his tone implies that marriage is for those who don't quite have what it takes to live the better life! (See 1 Corinthians 7.)

The season of "married without children" is also a special time to express one's design and grow. There is still time to serve others and to develop a career. Indeed, some couples I know have chosen not to have children because they felt so called either to certain forms of service or to their jobs. I believe this is a valid choice, though one that must be made after much prayer and thought.

The Seasons of Raising Children

The season of having children is largely a season of meeting needs. The needs change as the children grow, so raising children means passing through several different seasons. Debbie Barr, in her book, *A Season at Home*, suggests that the most important time for a "season at home" is the first year of a child's life. That is the period, studies show, when separation from the mother critically upsets the mother-infant bond, with apparently lasting effects.[2] Barr and others believe that the first year of life is the bare minimum of time when a mother should be at home full-time.

The next two years, from age one to age three, are also important. This is the period when children are still vulnerable to separation for more than a few hours at a time. Also, during this brief window of time children develop crucial abilities and inner qualities and have an insatiable desire to learn. They are so wide open to input that many moms are rightly wary of anyone else's doing the job. One mother of a two-year-old told me, "I feel good about my caregiver, but she and I differ on some things, and I just don't feel comfortable with the influences my son is exposed to." The ideal minimum, Barr says, is for moms to spend the first three years of their children's lives mostly at home (defined as not having outside child care for more than twenty hours per week).

Ages three to six constitute the "yellow light" phase of Barr's schema. This is a time of transition, when choices and options need to be cautiously made. During this time, children can tolerate longer separations from mom but still benefit greatly from her presence. (I might also add, for many moms this is the most enjoyable phase. I myself love this age group, and my child's needs aside, *I* don't want to miss them!)

The "green light phase," from age six and up, marks the season in which being at home may be less important to a child. This is a time when many mothers feel they have more time to pursue outside commitments. Some, whose design suits them best for nurturing, may elect to "go the second mile" and continue to be there for their children.

Seeing my life in terms of seasons helps me as I focus my life purpose to the circumstances at hand. Right now, I am in the "yellow light" phase. My life purpose of helping people develop their full potential is narrowed to doing that for my family members, and in a few other relationships in which God has put me. I also work, but my work is woven around the more primary needs of my family right now. As their needs change, I may be able to widen my efforts, or to redirect them in new ways.

The New Familism

Women who have opted to stay home for a season often feel they are in the minority, but in fact, many women are choosing that option these days. A subtle shift in values may be taking place. Many women have told me, "If you have chosen to become a parent, then you must take responsibility to raise your children."

Dr. Barbara Dafoe Whitehead, research associate for the Institute of American Values, believes that a cultural shift is taking place. "It is a shift away from the assertion of individual rights and toward a recognition of individual responsibility. It is a shift away from a preoccupation with adult needs and toward greater attention to children's needs. It is a shift away from a calculus of happiness based on individual fulfillment and toward a calculus of happiness based on the well-being of the family as a whole. This is . . . the new familism."[3]

The "new familism" is not really new; Christians who have known the value of family have always practiced it. However, it's encouraging to see that there is more support in the wider culture for the choice to stay home to major in parenting for a time.

Choosing to stay at home is a decision based on one's values. While I cannot tell you how long your "season at home" should be, I do want to give you some guidelines for deciding.

What It Takes

Strong desire and conviction. The main resource needed to make "a season at home" work is a strong sense on both your part and your husband's that this is the right thing to do. Arlene Rossen Cardozo, in researching for her book *Sequencing,* found (to her surprise) that the decision for the mother to stay home did not depend on the husband's income so much as the conviction that the mother should be with her own children.[4]

Financial planning. Finances are always a major factor. Losing your income will mean revamping your spending habits and reevaluating the values that underpin them. Money is more than a means of exchange of goods and services; it can mean security, opportunity, freedom. It tends to define social status.

Be honest about what money means to you. If you're now considering giving up your job to stay home with children, talk over with your husband what losing your income means to each of you. What would you have to give up? How willing are you to make those changes?

Taking time out from the workplace to stay home with children is easiest if you *plan* to do so. Many financial experts suggest a couple start living off the husband's income from the start and using the wife's income to pay off college debt, save for a down payment on a home, buy a car and furniture, and the like. This is good sense, but it doesn't always work out that way. Often a woman thinks she will want to continue to work after having children; it isn't until she thoroughly falls in love with her baby that she changes her mind. Or a woman may find that working full-time didn't strain the family until a second child came along; then she begins to reevaluate whether a season at home really would make the most sense for her and her family.

No matter what stage you are in, before making a final

decision, it's wise to first work out a realistic budget based on your husband's income alone. (For suggestions on some helpful tools for this, see the Resources at the back of the book.) If you don't have a realistic sense of your actual expenditures, keep track of every penny you and your family spend for two or three months. Then do a budget. Remember to *exclude* in your revised budget all your current work-related costs: child care, transportation, lunches out, business clothes, take-out/fast-food meals for when you're too tired to cook, taxes. (You may find that losing your income puts you in a lower income bracket.) Some women are astounded to see how much their net income shrinks when they figure this all out in black and white. One woman said, "When I realized that I was working four months for Uncle Sam, five months to pay child care, another two months to pay for work-related expenses, all of a sudden it didn't make sense. Only one month's worth of my paycheck was going toward improving our standard of living!"

Even if, after doing this exercise, you come up with a significant shortfall, don't despair. You may be able to implement cost-saving strategies. Or you may be able to earn that much money by working from home (chapter 10). Do your figuring, begin to live on a reduced budget for a few months as a trial, consider other options, and reevaluate.

Support. Besides a financial plan and conviction, to be happy at home you will need to find some outside support for your decision. The culture at large does not value full-time mothering. Just note the reaction when a first-time acquaintance asks, "And what do you do?" and you say, "I stay at home with my children." Usually the person will cock an eyebrow and quickly move on to someone "more interesting." (You might want to come up with some answers ahead of time to the question. I like the simple expression, suggested by Arlene Cardozo, "I'm mothering." It has an active, deliberate feel and tends to reinforce the whole reason for being at home: to consciously shape our children's world.)

Finding a network that reinforces your values may mean finding two or three other moms who are at home with young children (particularly good for Introverts, who like to develop in-depth relationships with a few), or finding a group to join (which may be most attractive to Extraverts). You may find people in your church, in your neighborhood, even in the park. Or you can contact a national group with local chapters, such as F.E.M.A.L.E. (Formerly Employed Mothers at the Leading Edge) or MOPS (Mothers of Preschoolers) International.[5]

One woman said she views herself as a professional—a professional mother. Her proof: "I am constantly reading to keep up with my field, I attend conferences on mothering, and I am a member of two mothering professional (and support) groups."[6]

A clear sense of how you will express your design in this area. Leaving a job to mother your children will involve a change in your own perception of who you are. If you have a clear sense of your design, that transition will be less traumatic.

The wonderful thing about being an at-home mother is that you can basically fit the job to your design. Think about all the possible things the job description might entail: mentor, disciplinarian, teacher, playmate, interior decorator, chief financial officer, repair person, purchaser, chauffeur, recreation coordinator-party planner, gardener, cook, wardrobe planner, organizer—to name a few.

As we saw with the job of parenting itself (which takes up a good deal of an at-home parent's time and energy), the job of being at home full-time can be shaped according to your design. Let's look at two women who have done just that.

Fiona: Shocked to Like Being Home

Fiona Gierzynski bustled around her kitchen as we

conducted our interview. My three-year-old son played with her children, ages three and two. Her oldest, Kyle, was in kindergarten at the moment, in the school just across the street. As we talked, Fiona made cookies, poured drinks, excused herself to discipline her kids for getting Play-doh™ in the living room, pulled out coloring books and crayons, and let the neighbor girl in to play. She picked up baby Wenona and nursed her at one point.

Fiona was an English major in college and started out teaching after graduating. But she didn't like it and switched to sales. She worked herself up the ladder until she reached an executive position, the kind where "you have to wear $300 suits," she says. She made forty percent of their household income but spent it all. "The job was so stressful, I was having nightmares about it," Fiona says. She was trying to get pregnant, unsuccessfully. The doctor told her to relax. Her husband, Paul, urged her to quit because she was driving him crazy. Fiona and Paul had already agreed that she would stay home when they had children: "We were firmly of the opinion that if you have children, one parent should be at home. Children should feel important to someone when they are young."

Fiona decided to quit her stressful job even before she got pregnant, figuring the stress might be preventing conception. "I gave my boss three weeks' notice and got pregnant in that same time period," she says.

She got a part-time job at a fabric store that gives employees a fifty percent discount on fabric. Since sewing was enjoyable to Fiona, she used that skill to further save them money by sewing curtains and all her maternity clothes. Once she had her first baby, she quit that job to stay home full-time—and to have three more children in rapid succession (the biggest gap between her children is twenty-four months).

Fiona says she did not expect to enjoy being at home with small children. In fact, she says she expected to hate it.

"My mom was home, and she hated it," Fiona says. "I expected to put up with being at home for the kids' sake." To her surprise she actually enjoys being home with her four children. She adds a caveat: "I'm not sure I would have liked it if I had done it earlier. I liked being an executive for a while. If I hadn't gotten it out of my system, I might have hated being at home."

Her comment dovetails with the findings of a 1984 study by the Center for Research on Women at Wellesley College. The study found that for women, the two primary components for satisfaction were mastery and pleasure. By mastery the researchers meant what makes a person feel like a valuable member of society and a person in control of her own destiny. And pleasure was defined as that which makes people find enjoyment in their lives. Most interesting was that the arena in which mastery was achieved (employment, marital relations, children) was not nearly as important as the fact of mastery itself.[7]

Yet, had Fiona discovered her design, she would have received plenty of assurance that she would like staying at home with young children. As we explored her early Satisfying Activities, teaching stood out clearly. "I was the type of kid who always got my homework done quickly, and then I was bored," she recalls. "Pretty soon the teachers caught on and started asking me to help the other students. So I spent most of my time in the early grades, first, second, third, fourth, helping the teachers teach the other kids. And I really liked that."

Fiona does that now, too, in her mothering. "I walk around in the grocery store with the kids, and I tell them I need four cans of beans, and they give me one. So I say, 'Okay, that's one. Now how many more do I still need to get four?' So I teach in everyday life, with all of them, I try to, and I try to make it painless. And I'll go off on tangents and discuss world events, all kinds of things at the drop of a hat."

Fiona's preferences are ESTJ. The Extraverted ("I'm always talking") and the Thinking side of her is obvious in what she shared. Her Sensing-Judging combination is also expressed in her well-ordered schedule: Mondays she does laundry, waters the plants, cleans her contacts; Tuesday she takes her children to various activities; Wednesday, she and the kids go to play-group, and she again washes diapers; Thursday is grocery shopping, Friday is the day to "hang loose" and visit with people, Saturday is chore day, and Sunday is family day. She hates housework but has a level of cleanliness that she insists upon and figures that she spends at least fifty percent of her time cleaning. Again, she has a schedule for when the vacuuming and floors are to be done. She also likes to bake and cook—tasks that often appeal to SJs, because there's a step-by-step sequence to the task, and there are tangible results of the labor.

With a clear preference for Extraversion, it's not surprising that Fiona enjoys spending time with her children. However, her SJ side often wins out: "One of my frustrations is that I'm always so busy, it's hard to find time to just play on their level, in their time frame," she says. She doesn't have any trouble taking them places, such as to the grocery store. "We have rules. The kids help me pack up the food. If they behave, they all get candy as a reward." (Note her Thinking preference showing itself again: She has no trouble pointing out the rules and enforcing the consequences—in this case, rewards for good behavior.)

Fiona's Extraversion also shows itself in the fact that she enjoys the noise and activity of having several young children around. In fact, she grew bored when she had just one. "I had so much energy, there wasn't enough for me to do with just one child. I think I would have obsessed over Kyle if he had been my only one."

Fiona's remark made me think that a preference for Extraversion or Introversion may well be a factor to consider when deciding how many children are right for a person. I know that, as an Introvert, I prefer to focus on one at a time. In a conversation with another Introverted mother over how far or close to space children, she said that she liked the wider gap because it allowed her to concentrate better on one at a time.

Fiona's Extraversion is also expressed in her need for validation from the outside world, especially since her mother often tells her how she is "wasting" her mind and her education. Her one outlet is involvement in F.E.M.A.L.E. (Formerly Employed Mothers at the Leading Edge), from which she gleans support and social relationships along with outside stimulation.

Fiona also needs some time to herself, of course, but that is one of the things she often sacrifices. Sometimes, late at night, she will either read or sew, both of which she finds satisfying. "But usually I'm too tired," she said.

Another area that gets short shrift for Fiona is time with her husband. She is militant, therefore, about a once-a-month date night. "The books all say do it once a week," she says, "but that's not practical for us. This way, we trade off baby-sitting with another couple, so we don't have that cost." She also trades baby-sitting services for other things and thinks that time away from the kids occasionally is essential to keep her sanity. And, she points out, you don't have to pay for it if you consciously seek people with whom you can trade services.

The hardest tradeoff for Fiona is not earning her own money. "I won't buy new underwear until what I have is falling apart. I guess it's because I think it's Paul's money, not mine. But Paul is my staunchest supporter: He's always telling me, 'Do you know how much it would cost to replace you?' I did figure it out once. I would have to make megabucks to cover child care for four children, plus hiring someone to do all the things I do around here." From this she gets some solace, but it's still hard for Fiona not to think of the money as Paul's, not hers.

As her children get older and need her less for hands-on help, it's likely Fiona will begin to get restless and need more outlets. That's part of her personal style, part of her design. At this point, Fiona is open-ended about when she will return to paid employment—maybe when her youngest is in first grade. Even then, she may go back into teaching so that she will be on the same schedule as her children.

Fiona is one example of a woman who has made the decision to sequence, and has molded the task to her personal style. By way of contrast, let's look at another woman, of a very different type, who is also at a different place in the sequencing process.

Debbie: Moving Toward "Something of Her Own"

Debbie Berkley is the mother of two teenagers, Peter, sixteen, and Mary, fourteen. She stayed home with them until they were in sixth and fourth grades, respectively. At that point she worked part-time at a local college, doing administrative work in the theater department, to earn money to go back to school for a doctorate degree. When I interviewed her, she had a year or two to go before finishing a Ph.D. in linguistics—something she had started before meeting and marrying her husband and then taking several years out to be a mom.

Debbie's fascination with language is a key part of her design. Her earliest Satisfying Activities involve playing around with sounds and languages. When she took a course in college in linguistics, she was amazed that one could major in this thing that she loved, and she was hooked. She knew that this was what she wanted to do for her life's work.

But then marriage and children came along, and Debbie knew she wanted to mother her children during the key years more than she wanted to pursue linguistics. Both Debbie and her husband, Jim, had moms who stayed home while they were young, then went back to school when the kids were in early adolescence, so to Debbie this was a pattern that felt natural.

With preferences for INFJ (Introversion, Intuition, Feeling, and Judging), Debbie approached the task of motherhood with dedication and a strong sense of its value. "I didn't have much trouble staying home because I really believed being a mom was creative and important—it takes a lot of thought." Though she had the social support of other moms—she was part of a Bible study group of other stay-at-home moms—she didn't need it as much as some Extraverts might. She focused on the task at hand, and found great challenge and fulfillment from guiding her children toward maturity.

However, Debbie still found ways to express two elements of her design—her fascination with language and her love for learning—even while she was home. She kept a diary for each of her children when they were very young, in which she recorded every new word they said that day. "I was probably more interested in their verbal development than most other moms are," she acknowledges. During nap times she taught herself New Testament Greek and Latin and reviewed the formal logic she had learned in her undergraduate studies. "That was my favorite part of the day."

Because of her strong sense that staying home was important and valuable, Debbie found it relatively easy to deal with the financial aspects of living on one salary. "We never felt squeezed financially because I've never craved a lot of things," she says. This, too, is true to her type: Introverted Intuitives, who have a rich inner life and who focus more on possibilities than present realities, tend to be less focused on possessions or their surroundings than their opposite types, Extraverted Sensors.

Debbie thinks a great deal about her mothering. She and her husband always limited the children's television viewing time, for instance, "for spiritual and intellectual reasons." They are strict in the sense that the children always have to let them know where they're going. Debbie has no trouble seeing each of her children as a unique individual, and she relishes the ways they are growing and developing. In talking with her, I sensed the quiet, intense dedication to her values that is characteristic of someone whose preferences are INFJ—she must believe in what she's doing to do it well.

Debbie says that one of the few things she feels bad about in her mothering is that she was not good at thinking up fun things to do. The neighbor kids never congregated at her house; her kids went to their friends' houses.

Her present lifestyle reflects both the struggles and strengths of her type. Going to school full-time takes up thirty to forty hours of her time; this leaves little time for much else besides school and the essentials of mothering. Debbie uses some of the monthly stipend to hire someone to clean her house, a task she always hated (as Intuitives tend to do); her Extraverted husband ferries the children to their various activities; and Debbie studies, cooks, and focuses on being available to talk with her children. She has given up volunteer activities to concentrate on her two present priorities, parenting and studying.

There is a certain joy that comes to Debbie in accomplishing something in her own right. "For a while I was the pastor's wife; now it's nice to have my very own thing, nice to have achievements in my own right." Sometimes she gets so caught up in her studies that she forgets to get dinner!

But one area she does not compromise in: her parenting. Debbie has found that teenagers require even more energy and creativity than young children. She worries that she could be a better mom if she were home more. "Don't assume that you can put your parenting on autopilot when your kids are teenagers," she warns. "They still take a lot of energy and creativity—and the worries are greater."

Different Styles, But Satisfaction Too

Debbie demonstrates a different parenting style from Fiona's. For Fiona, "being there" means physical presence and tending to her children's basic needs. To Debbie, "being there" includes that, but her focus is more on feeling emotionally and intellectually close to her children. She's thrilled at the questions her teenage son brings to her, though they're not always easy to answer. Debbie needs intellectual stimulation; Fiona needs to be able to control and organize her world. Two different people, two different designs. Both have found ways to express their gifts and strengths at home and find great satisfaction in doing so.

Now let's turn to you. Look again at the elements of your design. How much of that can be fulfilled at home? How can you redesign the job description of "at-home mom" to reflect who you are? What do you need to add to the mix to find a more satisfying balance?

In the next chapter we'll look at some tips for staying home—by design.

CHAPTER SEVEN
STAYING HOME—
BY DESIGN

I was at a meeting for new members of F.E.M.A.L.E., a support group for moms who have chosen to stay home. We had broken up into small groups of six or so, and were discussing how we felt about leaving our jobs to mother our children.

"The hardest thing about staying home for me," said Carla, a woman with a ten-month-old, "is that I no longer bring in a paycheck. It's not so much that we don't have that extra money, it's that I'm not *earning* it myself."

"That doesn't bother me so much," chimed in Patti, a petite brunette with dark eyes to match. "I just hate the structure of not having a job to go to. I'd sit around in my bathrobe all day if I didn't make sure I had someplace to go."

"I like being home," confessed Karen. "I don't miss my job one bit. The kids and I have loads of fun. I just wish I could get myself a little more organized around the house. Sometimes I get overwhelmed by all the things I have to get done."

"I like it too," said Lois, with a swing of her blond head. "Although I admit I'm a bit bothered by the fact that my husband doesn't do anything around the house anymore, like he used to when we were both working."

"I like being with my baby, but I also get lonely," Joan admitted. "I miss going into the office, being a part of things, you know?"

These women expressed some of the joys and frustrations of choosing to stay home with children. I like one of the "Baby Blues" cartoons: Toddler Zoe and Mom are in the living room amidst blocks, books, and rattles. Zoe says, "Da Da?"

"No, Daddy's at work, Zoe," Mom replies. "Daddy works in a big office where he has a desk and a computer and gets to talk to other adults all day long and go to nice restaurants for lunch with interesting people." Zoe, big-eyed, stares. Mom points to herself, eyes looking up, "Mommy had to put *her* career on hold while she just sits here watching you grow up!"

"Mama," Zoe says, giving her mother a big kiss.

Mom hugs Zoe and says with a big smile on her face, "Poor Daddy."

That captures it, doesn't it? Yes, we may put a career on hold. The rewards are unpredictable but so sweet when they come: an infant's big smile, meant for Mom alone; seeing a toddler take his first steps, hearing the first words and sentences; the preschooler's unexpected hug and "I love you"; the grade-schooler bursting through the door after school to tell all about her day; the teenager who unexpectedly opens up and shares a problem that's been bothering him—and actually asks for advice!

Years invested in the lives of your children are never wasted, no matter what you give up in terms of career.

The first phase of sequencing—staying home completely for a season, however long that season becomes—involves predictable satisfactions and frustrations, depending on the elements of your design. If you've decided to make this choice, or are considering it, knowing these frustrations and what to do about them will help you shape the job to who you are. Let's look at why women with different elements of their design choose to stay home and also at ways they can maximize their time at home according to their own gifts.

Personal Style

Extraverts. Janet Penley has studied why women elect to work or stay home, and she has found that many Extraverts decide to stay home because they want to reserve their first and best energy for their children. However, Extraverts need to also take some time to give themselves the outside stimulation and social contacts they need. Extraverts often have a lot of energy, and if they don't find enough outlets at home they may need to look to the community or church for additional ways to use their gifts. Isolation is the hardest thing about staying home for Extraverted moms. They feel restless at home and do best when they can find ways to get out and about, with and without children.

Extraverts may also suffer if they do not have peers who are doing the same thing and who can provide validation of what they're doing; Extraverts are susceptible to the opinions of others.

Introverts. Introverted moms often elect to stay at home because the task of juggling both work and family seems overwhelming. Introverts tend to feel there just isn't enough energy for home and work.

Because mothering is in itself an extraverted task, Introverts will need to respect the fact that their way of refueling is through taking time to be alone and to focus on their inner world. Just as Debbie Berkley used her children's nap times to pursue her own interests, Introverts need to see such time as a necessary way to replenish energy reserves. "Mom's night out" for an Introvert may not mean getting together with a group of friends but shopping by herself, curling up with a good book, getting together with her best friend, or finishing a project of her own (depending on her other preferences).

Sensors. Because Sensors focus on what comes to them through the senses, many of them are especially attuned to many of the tasks of homemaking. I have one Sensing friend whose home is a special delight. Her preferences are, in fact, ESFJ, and homemaking provides many opportunities to express her personal style. Her hospitality bespeaks her Extraversion and the personal warmth of a Feeler. Her home is beautifully decorated, full of interesting objects, clean and well-organized—marks of an SJ. Another friend, an ESFP, also excels in hospitality, an interesting home, and personal warmth, but she is less organized and more focused on having fun in the moment.

Sensors might focus on providing their children with rich sensory experiences, establishing family traditions, showing love in concrete ways such as cooking a special meal, always keeping the cookie jar filled, or sewing a special outfit.

Intuitives. The hardest part of staying home for Intuitives is the routine and mundane aspects of daily living. Intuitives have no trouble keeping "the big picture" in sight; it's the everyday stuff that drags them down. They may take on too much because they're not as adept as a Sensor in knowing exactly how much time household tasks actually take. Janet Penley suggests timing tasks and writing down how long it takes, for future reference (a suggestion I have found helpful).

Intuitives usually dislike housework, even if they are Judging types. (NPs, the Intuitive Perceivers, have an even worse time with the many details of housekeeping.) One INTJ woman I know says that even if it would mean eating beans and rice all week, she would do it in order to be able to pay someone else to clean her house. (In fact, this woman doesn't even own her own vacuum!) If an Intuitive can't hire out the work she hates to do, she may want to experiment with finding new and novel ways to do the mundane.

Intuitives are likely to approach the season at home as a time to learn all about children and parenting. They'll benefit from reading about child development and swapping information with other moms. Intuitives value their time at home as a growth experience for themselves. One mom told me, "I had a total personality change after I became a mother. It turned me into a much better human being." Though I don't know her preference for sure, I suspect it is Intuition.

Thinkers. Thinkers may elect to stay home because, as Fiona said, parenting is the most important job one can do. However, Thinkers may feel bored by very young children, who are not yet able to engage in much stimulating intellectual debate. If they have a clingy, dependent child, they may begin to feel trapped in their role.

Thinkers need validation for their competency, above all. This is seldom given in the task of parenting alone. That is why a good many Thinking moms, especially if they are also Judgers, tend to seek validation through employment. However, if you're a Thinker and you feel strongly about being at home with your children, there are other things you can do. There are plenty of opportunities in community work to gain experience, validation of your competence, and a sense of being useful and productive—with the added advantage of flexibility. (Most volunteer jobs are flexible in terms of hours and times you'll be needed.) Another alternative is to work out your own standards of judging how well you're doing, and ask your husband or a good friend to give you periodic "evaluations"—along with an appropriate reward, of course! In other words, if you're feeling frustrated at home because there are no objective ways to measure your performance, set up those standards yourself and ask someone to hold you accountable.

Feelers. Feeling moms stay home with their children

because they don't want to jeopardize their closeness with their children. It's probably hardest for a Feeling mother to turn over the care of her precious children to others. They are very aware of how much their children need them, and they relish the privilege that is theirs to meet that need.

Feeling moms can go overboard in the nurturing realm, however, as we saw in chapter 6. If you're a Feeler, choose one other thing that gives you pleasure, something besides parenting that you feel strongly about, and make sure you set aside regular time for involvement with that activity. Your children will thank you for it, believe me.

Judgers. People who prefer Judging like to maintain maximum control over their home life. They may not find it so easy to delegate to others, which common sense indicates would be a prerequisite for successfully juggling home and family. However, this very trait also leads to the frustration of being at home with young children: Judgers like to control and complete concrete tasks, yet with young children, there are constant interruptions, crises, and endless unfinishable tasks to attend to. The minute you get the house clean, in barges the dog and the kids, tracking mud. Your elaborately prepared meal is consumed in a few short minutes without comment, and you're faced with dirty dishes to clean up.

The Judging mom at home can deal with this frustration by making sure there is some place or project of her own that she can control, organize, and complete. This may be some household task such as sewing, or an outside responsibility. A Judger can also find balance by taking time to do some things that are not tied to finishing a job but simply to enjoyment, whether it's walking the dog, reading a magazine, or calling a friend.

Judgers may also find themselves getting too involved in what they want to finish that they forget to have fun. One INTJ mother of two young children is so goal-oriented that she calls herself "fun-impaired." If you feel this way, make it a point to find new ways to have fun with your children. After all, this is part of the reason you decided to stay home!

Janet Penley suggests taking the children out of the house, so you're not distracted by what needs to be done at home. Or introduce your child to what was fun for you as a child. "Especially with young children, it's easier for them to 'play' what's fun for you than for you to 'play' what's fun for them."[1]

For the Judger, especially if she's also a Sensor, straightening the house may be therapeutic. One INFJ mom told me she uses the time dusting and cleaning to reflect and gather her thoughts. Another, an ENFJ, does housework to rousing music and feels refreshed. A Judger might even think it's worth it to hire a sitter so she can clean the whole house! The sense of completion, of bringing order to the home, may well refresh her enough to feel like a worthwhile expenditure of time.

Perceivers. Those with the Perceiving preference may find the task of juggling and structuring work outside and inside the home too taxing, and thus may choose to stay home. One Perceiver told me, "I love to sleep in and to set my own schedule. Why would I want to go out and work?" Perceivers are also aware that young children are what speaker Bill Butterworth calls "slow-poke people in a hurry-up world." Perceiving moms feel uncomfortable pushing children into pre-set schedules too early in life; they themselves dislike too much structure and scheduling.

But the Perceiver at home may struggle with keeping her house organized and in order. She is the most likely to feel boxed in by the SJ approach I heard the other day on a radio program: Write all the tasks to be done on a weekly basis on a card, and every day to do the task for the day. A Perceiver might need to get organized more than anybody, but all the nice systems don't seem to work with her style. (I know whereof I speak, because this has been a constant struggle for me.) In this I have found Janet Penley's suggestion helpful: Start the day by writing down just two or three things that must be done or else things will fall apart. Keeping to the essentials will help a Perceiver to feel focused yet flexible to meet the challenges and opportunities of the day.

If a Perceiver can afford it, she might want to consider hiring help with housework as well. Many moms I talked to suggested teenagers, who can often clean a house for much less than the commercial housecleaners. (They may be your baby-sitters as well.)

Perceivers like their children to experience a wide range of activities, but they need to remember that usually this means some scheduling and structuring on mom's part as well. She should be realistic about her own ability to chauffeur her children here and there, perhaps limiting each child to one activity at a time.

Energized Skills

Being at home provides many opportunities to use a wide range of energized abilities. A very few, such as publicizing, selling, and promoting, may need another outlet, but most skills can find expression at home. One mother loves music and drama; she and her children stage plays at home and for the neighborhood, and she teaches piano in an expanding home-based business. Debbie Berkley satisfied her thirst for learning by teaching herself Greek during her children's nap times. I have shared how I use writing, learning, creating, relating, and reading in the context of the home to enhance my mothering and homemaking. I can see many other opportunities I haven't even begun to explore.

What about you? Can your favorite skills be adapted to your current situation? How? (If you are having trouble coming up with ideas, find an Intuitive friend and brainstorm.)

You'll also find yourself leaning heavily on your self-management skills while at home—and developing others as well! For instance, if you're naturally organized, you'll find this a real asset for your season at home. Creativity, self-motivation, patience, perseverance, the ability to see possibilities or to problem-solve—you'll have ample opportunity to hone any of these qualities at home. Build on your strengths and cut yourself some slack in areas where you may be weak.

Subject Matter

Besides your personal style, your design includes your preferred subject matter. Again, there are many ways to express this part of your design. Is it ideas? Learn about your new job as parent; discuss your findings with other at-home moms; keep a journal. Is it information? One mom I know is a wonderful resource for all kinds of information, from where the best resale shops are to how to remove crayon stains. Is it animals? You might consider breeding purebreds to earn some extra cash. Is it machines? You might want to take over maintaining the family car as well as all the other appliances and machines around the house. Is it figures? Take over the family budget and bill paying, do your own taxes—and maybe some friends' as well, in exchange for money or services. Is it money? You'll have ample opportunity, living on one income, to maximize your ability to "squeeze every penny until it screams," as one person put it.

Energized Outcomes

This aspect of design may or may not provide an easy fit with the tasks of being an at-home mom. My energizing outcome, to maximize potential, finds ample outlets at home. Not only can I help shape my child's character, but the whole challenge of maximizing our economic potential is simply endless. Finding ways to use up, fix, reuse, or adapt something so I don't have to spend money offers me plenty of opportunity to use this part of my design. Anyone living on a limited budget will find a myriad of ways to express such energized outcomes as *explore* (bargains), *pioneer* (new ways to make ends meet), *overcome* (the lack of funds), *prevail, meet the challenge* (of living on one income), *become proficient* (at cooking from scratch), or *gain response* (through her obvious devotion and importance to her children).

However, some people are energized by gaining recognition, or being the best (which necessitates outside confirmation of that fact), or progressing in some skill. People with these energized outcomes would probably find it harder to find satisfaction in the role of homemaker-mother.[2]

During the early sequencing years, such motivations may find their best expressions in an outside commitment that accommodates the limited time you want to give it. You might gain recognition by becoming the co-leader of a F.E.M.A.L.E. chapter, for instance, or to satisfy the need to be unique by starting an unusual service. (One woman, who I suspect has this energized outcome, started a local newsletter informing parents of happenings in the community particularly geared to families. She found a way to meet a unique need. People come to her for information they can find nowhere else.)

Energizing Circumstances

There are only a few energizing circumstances that do not lend themselves well to the home. Those who crave structure, deadlines, standards, or instruction may need some help along these lines. Again, maybe a woman with this motivation can ask her husband to help set some standards or deadlines. If she thrives under instruction, she might take a parenting class or become part of a parenting group. Elements like *meeting challenges, keeping active, adventure, flexibility, harmony*, all are easily found at home.

No Job Is Perfect

I'm sure I don't need to remind you that no job is perfect. There will be days when going to an office job, having defined coffee and lunch breaks, putting on makeup and nice clothes and leaving the chaos of home behind, sounds like a description of heaven. But even on those days, knowing your design can help. May I suggest that, when you face one of those days, you stop what you're doing as soon as you can, and find just *one* enjoyable thing that fits your design, and do it?

I've given you several suggestions of what you might find enjoyable. You may find it helpful to sit down with my list, and construct your own "de-stressor" list, based on your own design. Include all those things that give you pleasure, that fill you up, that relax you. It's best if you can include a wide range of possibilities: actions that take only two to five minutes, (for example, an Introvert indulging her mental wanderings for two minutes), things that take ten or fifteen minutes (for an SJ, for instance, straightening out a dresser drawer may restore sanity), pleasurable tasks that take up thirty minutes, and finally, activities that take up a whole block of time (such as browsing in a bookstore or library, or shopping, or taking a day trip).

Knowing your strengths and corresponding weaknesses can help you to keep a perspective on yourself. So you're a Perceiver whose house is not nearly as clean and organized as your neighbor, who is a Judger. Look at your strengths—you know how to have fun; your neighbor's children may not grow up with the memories of times at the park or just goofing around the backyard, as your children will. However, this doesn't give you an excuse to live in a pigpen. If you can't hire help, if you don't have a J in the family to delegate some cleaning and decluttering to, then pack up your own pride and go ask your J neighbor for some tips. Don't expect to reach her level of organization, and do expect it to be harder and take longer for you to make some positive changes. But keep at it. We're all trying to find some kind of balance, and we can learn from those who are different from us. Your neighbor may even start asking you how she can learn to relax more and be less compulsive about the house! (I have heard this exact exchange take place.)

Find God in the Hard Places

Also remember that it is often in our hard times, our points of stress and weakness, that God makes himself most real to us and does the most work on our character. Gail, a mother of two school-age children, moved with her husband, John, and family to Manila, in the Philippines. There she felt constantly frustrated but didn't know why. She sought some counseling and explored the various aspects of her design. She realized that she was constantly frustrated because nothing in her current situation allowed her to express her design. One of her energizing outcomes was to maximize efficiency. Yet in a city in which much of the time there was neither running water nor electricity, it was impossible to be efficient even in the daily routines of washing laundry or fixing meals that we in the United States take for granted. "It drove me nuts," she told me when we visited during a furlough.

"But you know what?" she added in an excited voice. "I have learned so much about God and myself from all this. I finally came to see that I was so performance-oriented, I really knew nothing of God's grace, deep down." Her drive for efficiency blocked her from realizing that she didn't have to perform to receive God's approval. Now she is learning about grace and finding some balance in her need for efficiency. She faces the return to Manila with an expectant sense of how God will use her strength, as it's being tempered by her new understanding of grace.

If you find yourself frustrated with being at home but

determined because of your values to make that a priority, you may have to practice self-denial for a few years. Rather than fight it, lean into it; open yourself to God and the lessons he may have for you. One mother, struggling with some of the same frustrations Gail expressed, said that breastfeeding her infant was a transforming experience. "At first when I started breast-feeding, I felt really impatient. It seemed to take so much time! If I couldn't maximize my use of that time, through reading or making business calls, I felt it was wasted. I'm so performance-oriented, I'm always trying to prove myself or earn someone's regard.

"Gradually, however," this woman continued, "I started to relax a little. I began to see that to be a good mother to my child, all I had to do was sit there, hold my baby, and the nourishment came from me to her without any real effort on my part. I was her world. She loved me, without my having to do anything to prove it first. I would sit there breastfeeding, pondering Psalm 131:2 and the image of me as a baby with God. It helped me see that I don't always have to *do* to be a good mother; sometimes it's just *being there* that is needed." For this mom, meeting her children's needs, though it stretched her uncomfortably at times, also stretched her in the direction of balance.

Even as you learn those lessons, however, I do recommend you find at least one way to express your design; it will help you be the best mother you can be. You can almost always find ways to express your design outside the home setting that won't mean compromising your values.

Something of Your Own

Even if you find that the home offers an outlet for many of your skills, a part of you may long for "something of your own." My friend Eve put it to me like this: "When I stayed home, suddenly there was nothing that only I could do, except nurse the baby. My husband can diaper or play with the baby just as well as I could, in his own way." Eve is a pianist, a professional accompanist. She longed to find that sense of identity through doing something only she could do.

There are many ways to foster "something of your own." One answer, of course, is to pursue a paying job of some sort. The next several chapters will examine this option. If you need money as well as an outlet, paid work is the sensible way to go. Most jobs, however, require a commitment you may not feel ready to make yet, and they may lack the flexibility you require. If you don't absolutely need the money, I urge you to look to community work to express your design outside the home.

The advantages of volunteer work are: It is flexible; you can determine when and how much you work; it is an excellent way to try new things and meet new people; and it is plentiful. Any number of churches, community, and nonprofit organizations need volunteer help. Volunteering is especially useful for those sequencing women who do not want to go back to their former paid professions but are not sure what they want to do when they are ready to get back into the workforce. Such women can try new things that are in line with what they've discovered about their design, in a low-key and nonthreatening atmosphere.

Volunteer jobs also provide you with a sense of satisfaction and accomplishment. George Barna, head of the Barna Research organization, estimated that volunteers represent perhaps two billion dollars *a week* of labor. As a volunteer, you are a vital part of the economic and social structure of this country. Even though you're not paid in cash, the experience you glean (that can be put on your résumé) can help you get a well-paying job when you feel ready to go back to paid work. It will also offer a positive answer to the question a potential employer may ask you someday: "What have you been doing for the last five (or seven or ten) years?"

Another way that sequencing moms can keep "something of their own" in the mix during their years at home is to keep a hand in their profession. Dress up and go out to lunch with former colleagues every two or three months, just to keep abreast of what's going on. Read the professional journals; keep up your membership in at least one professional organization. If you read something that might interest a former boss or colleague, tear it out with a brief note: "Saw this and thought it was interesting. What do you think? Give me a call sometime so we can talk." These actions demonstrate that you still care about your field, even if you're not active in it. When you're ready to go back, there will be a place for you to begin networking.

If you're entering a phase in which you realize you do have more time to devote to the achieving and job side of your design, the following chapters will offer you some ideas on what it takes.

CHAPTER EIGHT
PART-TIME AND PROFESSIONAL

*I*t's sort of both the best and the worst of two worlds, to work part-time," my friend Louise reflected. We were sitting in the park one perfect summer day, watching our sons play on the slides. It was one of those interludes we eagerly grasped: time to be with both our children and a friend.

It felt good to talk with someone who understands that working part-time has both distinct advantages and definite disadvantages. The advantages: We have time for days like today; there is just enough flex in our schedules to sometimes be spontaneous and call a friend to meet in the park when the weather is nice. (However, this date was prearranged, like most aspects of our lives.) We can do more with our families; we have time to keep friendships alive. Our lives are enriched by the fact that we have strong commitments both to our families and our careers.

But there is also a downside to that as well, we agreed. Sometimes we feel we don't do anything as well as we'd like. We say no to work opportunities, because it takes too much from family—and we watch colleagues pass us by. We wish we could be more organized at home. And sometimes it seems we too are always doing chores on weekends, rather than spending time having fun as a family.

Another reason that working part-time sometimes feels like "the worst of both worlds," we agreed, has a lot to do with expectations, our own and that of others. It's easy for us to expect ourselves to get as much done at home as women who are not employed—and others often unconsciously follow suit. Acquaintances may assume you are just as available as a stay-at-home mom to do everything from bake cookies to attending daytime Bible studies.

If you're considering working part-time, it's useful to first isolate your reasons for doing so. Your reasons, along with the strengths of your design, will point to the most effective strategies for getting part-time work and making it work for you. Perhaps you're currently at home full-time and looking to make a switch. Or you're working full-time and feeling the need to cut back. Maybe you're single and want some time to pursue more education and you can't afford to quit work altogether to go to school full-time. Whatever your reasons, they will make a difference in the approach you take toward getting part-time work and the options you can consider.

Reasons for Working Part-Time

1. *To find more balance in life.* "I know I would be a crazy person if I didn't work," Jan confided. "I wouldn't be a good mother, and would probably be divorced," she said half-jokingly. An INTJ with a strong need to validate her competence, Jan works part-time to express a part of her design that cannot be expressed at home. Balance for her is intellectual; work provides stimulation and the opportunity for her contributions to be recognized.

Joan worked full-time after her first baby was born but after three years decided that was too taxing for her. Her health began to deteriorate, and she realized that for her the juggling act was too stressful. Working part-time was a much better balance.

Arlene did not have children yet when she sought to reduce her work hours. Though it was in the back of her mind that working part-time would be a good setup once she and her husband did start a family, her main motivation was to get off the treadmill of her job at a major news magazine where the hours were long and the pressure intense. Arlene wanted to concentrate more on the quality of her work rather than the quantity.

Lisa is single, working a high-paying but stressful job in a marketing firm. She wanted to go back to school to get an M.B.A. but couldn't afford to quit work altogether. She went to her supervisor with a well-thought-out proposal on how to cut back so that she could go to school. The company agreed, even offered to pay part of her tuition.

Whether part-time means cutting back or adding to your hours of employment, it can be a good way to achieve more balance to your life.

2. *To keep your hand in your career.* Nancy is trained as a lawyer, and always assumed she would go back to work after she had her baby. However, her priorities changed. "I knew that I wanted to return to the legal profession, but being home to raise my daughter was my first priority," she says. Yet she knew that in order to return to law in the future, she would have to maintain her legal skills. She loves her work and is investing in her career while spending substantial time with her two children. Nancy feels she has found "a complete balance for my life" by working part-time.

3. *To ease back into the work world.* Joanne took twelve years off to raise children. After starting a national organization that gave her substantial work experience, Joanne felt ready to reenter the work world. However, like many women who have tasted the freedom of being one's own boss, Joanne didn't want to work forty hours a week for someone else.

Some of her most enjoyable volunteer work had involved doing desktop publishing, so she took some community college courses in desktop publishing and is launching her own new business, but on a very part-time basis.

Lisa, who stayed home for seven years, maintained the contacts she had with previous employers and colleagues during all those years. When a position opened up, one of these former colleagues told her about it. Lisa realized that she was ready for a job, but not full-time. She successfully negotiated to job-share the position.

4. *To provide financial stability.* Though committed to spending as much time as possible with her children, Karen and her husband found it impossible to keep up with the bills. She decided to look for work strictly to make money rather than to find fulfillment or enhance her career. Feeling uncomfortable with the idea of day care and realizing that the expenses of such would offset much of her paycheck, Karen decided to look for a job that she could work at night or on the weekend, when her husband could take care of their three children. A few years later, when the children were all in school, she found another job that coincided with their hours at school and gave her time off during the summer. Though Karen did look for jobs she could enjoy, her main criteria was not personal fulfillment but whether they would allow her the time she needed with family.

Before you make the decision to work part-time, decide what you want your focus to be—*why* you want to work. Is it to find balance? What kind of balance—more time for family or a personal life, more stimulation, more opportunity to use your gifts, a way to keep your hand in your profession, or simply a way to make money? Focusing on what you want out of the work part of your life will save you time and energy in your search.

Let's look at some women who have chosen various part-time options, and learn from them what we can about how to approach each option and make it work.

From Full-Time to Part-Time

If you are currently working full-time and considering making a switch to part-time, you may have some doubts and fears. The most logical place to start is with your current job: Does it lend itself to a part-time schedule? How do you convince your supervisor or company to allow you to do it? What's the best way to go about making the switch?

The jobs that lend themselves to part-time schedules include the following characteristics:[1]

1. *Multiple skills required in the same job.* For instance, an editorial position I held required me to edit assigned columns and articles, write articles, generate ideas, and proof galleys. Any of these functions could be handled by the same person, or delegated to freelancers, or divided among two or more workers.

2. *Independent or project-oriented positions.* Stephanie Rens-Domiano's work as a professional researcher is an example of this kind of work. She works independently on projects that don't involve other people and their schedules. Andrea is a radio producer and host. Aside from the three hours she does her live call-in show from the studio, she can work the other parts of her job—setting up guests for the show, for instance—from home, on a flexible schedule.

3. *Peak work loads.* Julie, an accountant, works seasonally, at tax time. Some positions deal with the public and have heavy business during certain times of the day; those hours can be filled in by professionals who work only those hours.

4. *High-stress positions.* In jobs where the individual is subject to constant demands, such as social workers or

teachers, there may be more openness to reduced hours or sharing jobs.

5. *Scarce job skills.* Systems analysts, electrical engineers, and those with other kinds of technical job skills that are scarce may have more bargaining power in negotiating reduced hours.

6. *Deadlines known well in advance.* Situations in which work can be planned weeks or months in advance, such as desktop publishing, graphic design, or editorial work, can be managed well under a part-time schedule.

7. *Creativity a key component.* In jobs that require constant creativity, such as writing or public relations, a shorter work week can actually increase productivity.

8. *The goals are clear and can be quantified.* Sarah Wagner is a sales representative for a communications firm. She and her company set her sales goals, and she is responsible for meeting those goals. The pay is based on how she meets her goals, not on how many hours she works.

Identify those things you currently do in your present job, or would like in a part-time position. How does your list compare with the eight characteristics mentioned above? For those characteristics that do match, describe how the various job functions might be split up and handled by you or others.

For example, when I was considering a proposal to make my full-time editorial position part-time, I came up with the following list:

—Some columns could be delegated to freelancers or other editors; I could continue the columns that I did the best.

—Articles could be done as assigned.

—Proofreading could be delegated or sent out to free-lancers.

—I could make sure I attended all ideas meetings.

Get down on paper the specifics of how you would design or redesign your part-time job. If your current position does not lend itself to a part-time schedule, then you may want to read the advice I give to those who are reentering the work force. But don't close your options off too quickly with your current employer. After all, you are a known quantity. If you've proven yourself valuable, you have some currency with which to buy what you want.

How to Approach the Employer

If you want to convert your full-time position to part-time, first of all you have to convince your employer that it is in the company's best interest to let you do so. In the current corporate climate of "downsizing" and "right sizing," this may be easier than it has been in the past.

Step One: Establish your worth. All the success stories of people who have reduced their work hours were based on a proven track record. Joy Cohan quit her job when she and her husband relocated for his job and she had a baby. She didn't plan to work, but her former boss approached her with a proposal to work part-time from her home. "I had invested a lot of training in Joy," her boss explains, "and I didn't want to lose her. I had a very high regard for her and her work." Sarah Wagner also paid her dues before she persuaded her employer to let her work mostly from home after she had her baby. Once you prove that you can do the work and are committed to your career, you have some clout. As Joy's supervisor put it, "It's in the [employer's] interest to look for ways to keep the investment [in personnel] active."

But what if you have felt overwhelmed and the quality of your work has suffered because of the imbalance between work and family? This happened to Kirsten Nelson, a television journalist. After she had her baby, she worked full-time on the night shift. It was too much for her. The quality of her work suffered. When she approached her boss about a change, the supervisor said, "I don't care about your personal life. If you can't hack it, get out." Kirsten did quit, but ironically, her former boss kept hiring her back on a freelance basis.

However, Kirsten's story has a happy ending. She found a job, working one day a week, filling in for someone on maternity leave. Once her foot was in the door, she was in a position to both prove herself and to hear about other jobs that opened up. When she heard that the company had five shifts available for which they planned to hire freelancers, Kirsten suggested to another woman that they propose a job share. That job has worked out quite well, providing a way for Kirsten to continue to do work she loves, earn a good paycheck, and allow her plenty of time with her two young children.

Step Two: Network with other part-time professionals. Before you approach your supervisor, find other part-time professionals either in your company or in a similar company with a similar job. How did they go about getting their positions? Who approved the move? How did they structure the job? Find out the specifics so that you can use their success stories as examples. If possible, you might even ask if their supervisors would be willing to talk to your supervisor.

Networking may also link you up with someone else who is looking for a similar option. If the person's skills would match up with yours, you can propose a job share as Kirsten did.

Step Three: Construct your proposal. If you don't have a clear picture of just how your job may be restructured, keep a daily log for six to eight weeks of every major category of task you do. (This is also a good time to evaluate how much you enjoy each activity and how well it lines up with your design.) Keep the tasks you enjoy; think through how less enjoyable tasks may be handled in a way that's acceptable to your employer. What you are constructing is a new job proposal for yourself.

As you do this, be very clear in your own mind how many hours you want to work. A job log will help you know exactly how much time it takes to do each task you want to keep.

Step Four: Anticipate your response to your employer's objections. Imagine that you are the boss, whose main concern is to get the job done as efficiently as possible. What would your concerns and objections be? Talk to trusted colleagues for their perspective. Do some research about the benefits to companies of retaining proven part-time professionals.[2] For each argument, come up with a sound, strong counterargument. Role play with a friend or spouse until you feel comfortable and confident in presenting your proposal.

If your proposal is not accepted, you will need to pursue other options if you are really convinced that this is the right thing for you to do.

Finding a Part-Time Job

If you're reentering the workforce, or otherwise looking for a part-time job that suits your needs, you need first of all to know what you want. If you're not sure of that, I suggest you do two things: Go back to your design assessments and isolate the particular skills you want to use. Then start talking to people who are doing what you think you might want to do, or who are doing something related to what you want to do. To your list you might also add women who have moved from full-time to part-time (if that is your issue) and women who are working part-time at a company you might want to work for, even if they are not doing what you want to do. In that case, you are looking for information on how you might get hired part-time in a professional capacity.

Make a list of these contacts' names, addresses, and phone numbers. Then, either write to them or call them on the phone, depending on what you feel most comfortable doing. In your letter or call you will briefly explain that you are at a transition point in your life and are exploring your options. You have some idea of what skills you would like to use but are not exactly sure what kinds of jobs match up. You are fascinated by what your contact is doing and wonder if she would be willing to spend a few minutes sharing what she's doing. You might want to invite her to lunch or breakfast (you pay, of course), or just ask for ten minutes of phone time (if you don't know her at all, or if this is so new to you that you can't imagine inviting a stranger to lunch).

In your information interview, *do not* take along a résumé. You are not yet looking for a job. If the person asks for one, say, "I didn't bring one along, since I'm not really looking for a job yet, but if you like, I'll be happy to send you one." What you want to do at the interview is find out what this person does, how she got the job, what her background is, what she likes about the company, what opportunities she sees in her company, and anything else you want to know. What you want to communicate about yourself is that you are bright, you have interests that mesh with hers, that you have gifts you believe in.

This kind of "networking" by simply talking about areas of mutual interest is the least intimidating way to begin. And you never know where it may lead. As I have done this, each person I talk to has opened up to me her whole network of people who are also interested in the same thing. And so your network grows. Richard Bolles says that it takes about seventy eyes and ears to find a job. Once you do know what you want, you can go back to these people, who will already feel they know you, and tell them what you want. Then they can be looking and listening.

Knowing what you want is something you have to communicate at some point. And don't be afraid to be up-front about the fact that it is part-time work you're looking for. To give you some idea of some of the different approaches to securing part-time professional work, let's look at how four different women approached their job search.

Part-Time Professional: Stephanie Rens-Domiano

Stephanie Rens-Domiano had been a post-doctoral fellow in pharmacology for three years. Her original plan was to secure a faculty position at a university, which would allow her to teach and do research. She took three months' maternity leave after her baby was born, then worked full-time for seven months. When her husband was transferred for his job, Stephanie had to leave her job. She spent four months at home with their baby, and that made her realize that working full-time would not give her the time she wanted at home with her child. "There's a lot of expectations put on you prior to achieving tenure status," she says. "I was questioning how it would affect life at home if I worked full-time. I was weighing what's the impact at work against what my impact at home would be."

Stephanie decided to talk to people about other options in her field. She attended a national meeting of professionals and intentionally talked to people who were in Chicago, where Stephanie and her husband were about to move. "I talked with a University of Illinois-Chicago faculty member, who was particularly sympathetic and steered me to the right people to talk to. The more I talked with him and others about my goals, the more part-time sounded like the right option. People gave me their reflections on working and family and how the whole field is evolving."

One of the people Stephanie met was a woman who had secured a grant that would allow someone to do research part-time. "In talking with her we picked a project that could be done part-time," Stephanie says. Stephanie landed what she wanted: a part-time job in her field.

Note how Stephanie got her job in a field in which part-time work is relatively rare. She investigated the options and decided what she wanted to do (part-time research work). She actively sought people who could advise her. She was candid about both her goals and her qualifications. Her networking paid off in a job that she says is perfect in many ways.

Not that she isn't making some sacrifices; professionally, she has put herself on a much slower track. "Most of the [research] grants are available for full-time work," she explains. "It hurts me professionally not to be writing my own grants and getting my own support. When you go back to find a position as a faculty member, you need a track record of getting grants. Also, I'm not getting published as much as I should. Working two days a week, I'll be lucky if I get one article a year published. Normally a post-doctoral fellow would publish two or three."

However, Stephanie is at peace for now. At this point in her life working two days a week is perfect for both her and her family, in terms of balance. She loves her work. Her child seems to be thriving at the day care center she attends those two days. Though the pay is not wonderful, the opportunity to keep current with her skills and with contacts in her field makes it a good professional investment in her future.

Starting Over: Nancy Aliquo Long

Nancy Aliquo Long is another example of someone for whom networking led to opportunities she hadn't thought of. Nancy and her husband are both lawyers. She had done litigation for three years before she and her husband moved to Washington, D.C. She was pregnant at the time, and no one would hire a pregnant lawyer. After the baby came, she enjoyed being at home. Soon, however, it became clear to her that if she wanted to return to law at some point, maintaining her legal skills was a must.

While taking a bar review course so she could pass the

bar exam in the new state, she met a man who had been a solo practitioner; he was taking the exam in order to become a partner in a firm. Nancy began doing volunteer work for local bar associations, community organizations, and business-related organizations. She invested time and money into seminars that would qualify her to practice a new area of law—business law—that she could do from her home.

At one point, the man she met at the bar review suggested that she could become a solo practitioner by developing her own client base. "I had never thought of that," Nancy says. "He said, 'How would you like to be affiliated with the firm?'" It became a perfect situation for Nancy: She works two days a week at the firm but for her own clients. She pays a percentage of her salary to the firm in exchange for using the office, the support staff, and equipment. She is able to put the firm's name on her business card, which lends her credibility and attracts clients. She also maintains a home office.

Nancy says that networking has been *essential* to developing her successful practice. The volunteer work enabled her to make contacts and prove her skills. She is still active with local bar associations, community and business organizations.

Networking is also key in finding good child care. Through talking to other moms and joining a baby-sitting co-op, Nancy found good child care for those two days she is in the office. She works a few hours at night, either from home or out of the office, and her husband takes over the bedtime routine. She does housework on her nonwork mornings or not at all; she is adamant about spending the weekends doing fun things as a family, not chores or work.

"I am not making a tremendous amount of money, and I probably will not become a partner in a large law firm," Nancy says. "However, I am developing a law practice for my future, and I am still able to spend three days per week (plus weekends!) with my four-year-old daughter and my newborn. I believe that I have found a complete balance for my life."

Job Sharers: Christine Barrows and Dana Rollins

Christine Barrows has done it all in her career: worked full-time, freelance, part-time in a job-share position, and then back to full-time. When her two children were of preschool age, she worked from home, doing freelance projects for her former employer, a publisher of educational materials. However, she found freelancing very stressful. "Looking back," she says now, "it would have been much easier if I had had child care." Working twenty to thirty hours a week without child care meant working every possible moment that the children didn't need her. That, and the isolation, wore her out. Had she known her design then, she would have realized that she thrives in a team environment and is drained by working alone. She discovered these things instead through hard experience.

Dana Rollins was a friend who also worked at the same company Christine did. In fact, they had both had the same job at different points. Dana's child was one year old when Dana heard that the company was planning to hire someone for the very job both she and Christine had once held. It was a management job, but the more Dana thought about it, the more a job share with Christine made sense to her. She asked Chris if she was interested. She was. They did their research, showed why they were more qualified than anyone else, and explained in detail how they would divide up the job. They convinced the company to hire them.

For both Dana and Chris, the job worked out well. Dana enjoyed the people contact and being part of a team, the regular job schedule, and the authority of her position. ("Before, as a freelancer, I felt I had all the responsibility but none of the authority," she says.) The two worked well together, for a number of reasons. First, their personalities and skills complemented each other. Then, too, they were very committed to making it work. They took pains to communicate with each other, to be flexible (which meant, among other things, being willing to take calls at home when they were "off duty"), to be there when needed. Dana believes the company benefited greatly: "They had fresh blood and fresh enthusiasm mid-week." The job-share situation lasted for eighteen months, when Christine added some responsibilities and worked full-time. Dana stayed with her part of the job for another nine years.

Their advice for anyone who wants to job share:

1. Find the right person, someone whose skills and personality complement your own. Dana says that she and Chris were never in competition because their strengths meshed so well. You might want your potential job sharer to do a thorough skills analysis, akin to what you did in chapter 3.

2. Make sure you both share the same commitment to the job. "You need to be willing to go the extra mile, to take calls at home when you're off-duty, to make it work," Dana says. "I guess that's the difference between a career mindset and a job mindset." If both of you are using the job share to further your career, you will be more willing to make it work. By the way, it's also essential to demonstrate your commitment to the company.

3. Do your homework. Chris and Dana researched and networked with other successful job sharers in their city, asking them for advice. They also asked those people if they would be willing to talk to management about how and why it worked well. They cited their research in their proposal.

4. Prepare a well-thought-out proposal, complete with answers to anticipated objections. "Think of the job proposal as a job application," Dana advises. "You have to sell yourselves, individually and as a team." In

doing so, play up the years of combined experience you both bring; your track record; the way your strengths complement each other. In your proposal you should also detail exactly when each of you will work, what you will do about meetings, how you will communicate with each other, and the like.

Job sharing is slowly becoming a more acceptable option, but companies still tend to take it on a case-by-case basis. Like any innovative approach, it works best when you already have a relationship with an organization and if that organization has a proven track record of some flexibility in job options.

Part-time work may well offer you the best of both worlds. Many women have found it so, and say they will never return to full-time work again; part-time affords them the kind of balance they want. However, as with any option, there are trade-offs.

Possible Trade-offs of Part-time Work

Less pay, few if any benefits. Many of the part-time jobs available are neither challenging nor lucrative. If all you need in a part-time job at the moment is some social contact and a few extra dollars, part-time jobs abound. Fiona worked part-time in a fabric store so she could buy fabric at a discount when she was pregnant. She made all her maternity clothing and some baby clothes. Another woman, who worked from home, decided to supplement that by working a couple of nights a week at a dress shop. She enjoys clothing, and the store discount helped her pull together a wardrobe that she could not otherwise have afforded.

Going from a full-time job to part-time hours usually means a cut in pay, but not always. Sarah, a sales person for a communications company, makes a full-time salary on part-time hours. She and her company agree on her sales goals, and the company doesn't care how little or few hours it takes her to meet those goals. Remember that, even if the salary is less, often expenses are also less.

Some companies prorate benefits, so that you do receive some. Most don't give any benefits to part-timers, however. If you are not covered under a spouse's company plan for insurance, the loss of benefits may prove prohibitive.

Full-time expectations. One of the potential pitfalls of part-time work is that you can easily end up doing full-time work for part-time pay, especially if you have cut back from your full-time job or if you job share. It may be especially difficult for Intuitives or Perceivers to accurately assess how much time a task will take. One way to handle this is to keep track of how much time it takes to do your main job tasks. If you find yourself consistently working too much, you either have to renegotiate the job to reduce hours or get compensated for your extra time, or find some way to delegate more, or cut back.

Setting limits also applies to any outside activities you take on. I like what career counselor Richard Hagstrom advises: "Your job plus one other major activity (requiring up to ten hours per week), is about all anyone can handle comfortably." By this formula, a part-time job plus mothering is more than enough for most people. Be realistic about what else, if anything, you can take on.

Most of the women I interviewed said that they gave up being on church committees or being involved in community activities when they started working again. This can cause guilt, but it's really a matter of effectiveness. If you feel that employment and mothering are the tasks for this particular season of your life, then concentrating on these forms of service need not cause guilt.

Falling out of touch with the office "loop." When I worked part-time in an office (same office, different department from where I worked before), I felt I did not have time for much office chitchat. But I also realized that it really is important to stay tuned to the office grapevine. Talk to co-workers on your time off, or schedule short breaks during the day to keep in touch. It's a fine line to walk, I know, as you're trying to prove you're serious. But it's also important to stay informed and to make others know what you're doing as well.

Not being taken as seriously as before. When you don't work full-time, many managers assume you're not really serious about your career. Let them know you are serious by talking openly about your goals. When Kim went part-time, she restated her career goals in her proposal and spelled out how she would meet them. Not only is her career intact, but she also received a healthy raise.

Higher child-care costs. I have found that part-time child care is higher, proportionately, than full-time. At one center, the full-time costs for a three-to-five-year-old was $103 a week, or $21 a day; two days a week costs $53, or $26 a day. Also, part-time care is sometimes harder to find, whether in a center or with a family day-care provider. Some alternatives for part-time child care are: finding a relative or neighbor who is willing to take on that responsibility; swapping with another mom who works part time on alternate days; joining a babysitting co-op; finding a reliable college student or teenager.

Jobs not available in your field. Some jobs, more than others, lend themselves to part-time. If you do not think your field has openings for part-time workers, I suggest you do some research. Through professional organizations, ask if anyone is successfully working part-time. Check out organizations such as the Association of Part-Time Professionals (see appendix B).

You may find, after researching and networking, that you are more interested in the prospect of working from home. This can be done in any capacity: working from home for an organization, as Sarah the salesperson does; starting your own business; or freelancing or consulting, building your business.

Working from home successfully requires a high degree

of motivation, a clear knowledge of your energized abilities and self-management skills, and support from family and a network. Many start their businesses because they want to work part-time, on their own terms. In the next chapter we'll explore the special dynamics of working from home.

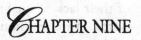

CHAPTER NINE
WORKING FROM HOME

*I*t's being called the "New American Dream," the answer to the work-family tension, the wave of the future in terms of how business is being conducted. An estimated twenty million households had some kind of income-producing home office in 1991, up from fifteen million households two years before.[1] According to the U.S. Department of Labor Women's Bureau, there are three million self-employed women in the U.S. Many of these are women who made their decisions based on family needs.[2] One national survey of people who work at home reported that nearly a quarter (twenty-two percent) of all working women work out of their homes—mostly in order to be with their children.[3]

On the surface, working from home seems like a perfect solution for women who want to or need to work for pay while their children are still at home. It can also provide an income source for the woman who took time off from working to raise a family. Many employers still do not view women who have been at home exclusively for a number of years as having "marketable skills" unless they have somehow actively utilized those skills. Home businesses can be a way to use the many skills developed over years of homemaking.

Other women hate the corporate world and dream of getting out on their own where they can call the shots. Or they hit the proverbial "glass ceiling" beyond which they cannot

135

rise either because of their lack of qualifications, life circumstances, or the corporate culture. Is a home-based business the ideal solution for them?

While no solution is ideal, a home-based business does offer distinct advantages to women in each of these circumstances. The advantages seem obvious: more time with the children; more control over your work; fewer interruptions; less time spent commuting; less money spent on lunches out; flexibility, and the ability to set your own hours; earning your own paycheck; an opportunity to continue your career, or start a new one; opportunities to minister; a sense of accomplishment and purpose; and potentially more money and opportunities than you can earn by working for someone else.

However, there are also distinct disadvantages, which are often glossed over in all the talk about how home-based businesses are the wave of the future, the answer to the mother who needs to or wants to earn money. Even some of the advantages mentioned above often harbor hidden pitfalls.

To decide if this will suit you, you need a clear sense of your own design, including your skills, gifts, and circumstances, and a realistic picture of what working from home really entails—especially if you have children.

Ways to Work from Home

Technology has afforded many new ways to work from home. Joy lives in Northern California as a sales rep for *Personnel Journal*, which is located in Southern California. She services her accounts mostly over the phone, although she does travel some. A typical day involves communicating with clients from her home office, via phone and fax machine. She uses her computer to keep track of accounts. The company paid for her office equipment as part of her compensation package.

Joy is an example of someone who proved her value at a

company before she moved to part-time, home-based work. She works from home *for* someone. Her situation is somewhat unique in that she is considered an employee, even though she is not based in the office. Most home-based workers who work for someone else are independent contractors who must pay their own Social Security taxes and do not receive any company benefits, such as paid vacation or sick leave, health care, or inclusion in pension programs.

Another way to work from home entails work done partly from home, partly somewhere else. Sarah sells ad space from home but goes into the office one day per week. Karen does her work mostly from home, transcribing for a local court reporting service, but she does pick up and deliver assignments twice a week. Other popular businesses are those that rely on home parties for customer contact, such as selling cosmetics, Tupperware, or toys. One advantage to working from home but linked up with a larger company is that you don't usually have to start from scratch in getting work, or in knowing how to market. For instance, Tupperware, Avon, and Discovery Toys all give training on how to get customers and run the parties. Because Karen works for someone else, she is assured a steady supply of work and can plan accordingly. Sarah feels connected to her office and colleagues.

When most people think of home-based businesses, however, what comes to mind is work done entirely at home. Providing day care, tutoring, making crafts, using the computer or phone are all examples of this kind of home-based business.

In fact, almost any skill or idea can be turned into a home-based business. Chicago resident and single mom Diane Rossi got her idea from listening to her neighbors arguing about who would pick up after the dog that had left a winter's worth of waste in the backyard. She began her business, "Have Doggie, We'll Doo!!" (slogan: "We pick up where your dog left off"). For thirty-seven dollars a month, Rossi's company offers clients a weekly cleanup visit from a "canine waste technician" equipped with a scooper. Business peaks in the spring, when many people order one-time service, but Rossi and her partner do steady business year-round. Though people thought her business a joke in the first year or two, Rossi has proven them wrong. It took two years to get to the point where she is now, able to support herself and two children on her income from the business, but she is doing it. The best thing was that she could limit her work outside the home to those hours her children were in school, so she was always there when they were home.

Diane Rossi proves that the idea for a home-based business can come from almost anywhere. However, making the idea succeed takes certain qualities and a particular plan of action. If you're considering starting a business or transferring your current job to a work-at-home arrangement, the following steps should prove helpful.

Step One: Look to Your Design

Your design will give you two crucial pieces of information: what you want to do in your business, and whether you are cut out for working from home.

In deciding what you want to do, look to your Satisfying Activities for ideas. What have you enjoyed doing and done well in the past? Look to your past work or volunteer experience. Mershon Shrigley realized that writing and putting together newsletters was something she had thoroughly enjoyed, and built on that to launch a successful marketing service.

Also consider your hobbies. Is there anything that can be turned into a money-making operation? Patti Khadkhodian always enjoyed sewing. She began sewing personalized bibs for friends who were having babies. People loved the bibs. She spoke at a play group and did a survey as to how many people would be interested in buying personalized bibs. She received a good response, and her business, Bibs Unlimited, was launched.

Another place to begin is to ask what needs do you see in your community that are not currently being met well. When Barbara Burns moved out to the Chicago suburbs, she noticed that her town and the surrounding towns were no longer small towns but were still functioning as small towns. There were lots of activities offered for families but not enough people knew about them. "People needed to know what's going on before it's going on," she explains. So she drew upon her background in business (she was trained as a CPA), and her Extraverted, can-do nature, began researching and networking, and created a newspaper called *The Family Connection*. The newspaper offers her the variety she always craved—she does everything from setting the budget to writing to delivering the newspaper to libraries, park districts, and other community centers. Her daughter, Katie, is four, and Barbara works three days a week while Katie is cared for by a friend who does home day care.

So in deciding what to do from home, make sure you choose something you love to do. The work itself should use at least one of your top five skills, and preferably more.

But there are other elements of your design that are just as crucial to look at. What about personal style? If the work requires you to work exclusively at home for long periods (writing, sewing), are you an Introvert? Conversely, if the work calls for extensive marketing and selling (all businesses call for some), are you an Extravert who will enjoy this? The Introvert/Extravert preference, along with your energized roles, are potentially very important. If you thrive on the stimulation of the outside world, you may well end up feeling cut off and too isolated at home. You will have to find some way to include enough people-contact to keep your energy flowing.

Even Introverts, however, can find working at home too

isolating. When Christine Barrows worked from home as a freelance editor, she felt too isolated. Though she is an Introvert, she is energized when she can work as part of a team. She felt cut off while at home. It was only when she moved into an office situation, where her efforts could be teamed up with that of others, that she began to find full satisfaction in her work. "Freelancing worked for me for a while, but it was never ideal," Christine says.

I, on the other hand, find working from home suits me quite well. I am an Introvert who thrives when I have several hours to play with ideas and get them down on paper. But I also need people-contact for stimulation. I have a few friends I can call, some of whom are writer friends who give me a sense of collegiality. I listen to the radio and read for outside stimulation and a sense of connection to the world. I have lunch with friends and former colleagues every so often. And I get to interview people about their lives. I don't feel isolated at all. In fact, I probably now have a wider network than I did before, when I worked in an office.

Look too at the "energizing outcomes" and "energizing circumstances" part of your design. Does the work you are thinking of doing match your design? If you're not sure, find people who are doing what you are considering. Ask them what they do, why it works for them, what problems they've encountered, and how they've dealt with those problems.

Working from home requires a certain set of self-management skills. You have to be a self-starter, able to either motivate yourself or know how to set up the conditions that motivate you. It also really helps if you have a high tolerance for stress and the ability to take risks. You also need to be able both to negotiate—to let your husband, children, and perhaps employer know what you need—and to "network," that is, let others know what you're doing. You need to be both organized and flexible. You need to be able to set clear priorities and stick to them, and to say no to things that come up that would eat away at your time. You need to feel entitled to work, and to believe in yourself and your idea. Think of Diane Rossi and her dog-cleanup business. For two years people laughed at her. But she knew that there was a need, and she believed in her ability to make the business work.

Step Two: Decide How Much You Can Invest

A home business can take over your life (as I'm finding). Opportunities come up, you feel you can't say no, and before you know it you're in over your head. Or, on the other hand, you may start a home business with a goal of needing to make a certain amount of money and find that the only way to meet that goal is to work full-time. That's fine if you have the time, but not if you are working from home so that you can be available to your children.

Realistically, most businesses started from scratch do not turn a profit for two or more years. There are many exceptions to this, but it's easy to be unrealistic about the amount of time and money needed to make a business a success. Realize that a home business will always take more time and money than you think.

Before you make the plunge, realistically assess both the time and the money and other resources needed to launch your business. Make sure that you are able to set the hours. Being firm about this in your own mind from the beginning will help you circumvent one of the major pitfalls of a home-based business, as we'll see.

If you don't have a clue as to how much time, money, or resources you need, don't skimp on the next step.

Step Three: Research Thoroughly

Before you invest any money or significant amounts of time in your proposed business, do some research. If you're considering bringing all or part of your current job home, talk to people who have done that. Check out your library for books on entrepreneurship, home businesses, finance, marketing. Read books like *Working from Home* by Paul and Sarah Edwards, which is very complete; *Homemade Business* by Donna Partow, and *The Part-Time Solution* by Charlene Canape, which contains an excellent chapter on working from home.

If you're planning on converting your current job to a work-from-home arrangement, find out if the company allows work-at-home. (Or, if you're planning to find such a job, find out which companies allow this arrangement.) Realistically assess whether the job lends itself to being done from home. Jobs that involve information processing, or that deal with finance, or that are creative (graphic artist, photographer, illustrator, decorator), and jobs that deal with clients (psychologist, lawyer, accountant, social worker), all lend themselves well to a home-based office. Write up a detailed proposal, pointing out why you are a good candidate for working from home and answering any objections your employer may raise. (For instance, if you're fairly social and your employer wonders whether you will feel too isolated at home, suggest that you come in one day a week to attend meetings and keep in touch with the other staff.) It's probably also a good idea to mention your child care plans, which will assure your boss that you do seriously intend to do your work.

If you're planning to start your own business, you have even more research to do. Who exactly is your market, the organizations or individuals that would pay for your product or service? How can you reach them? Who is already doing what you're planning to do? Can the market handle another business of this type? Talk to others who are doing what you plan to do, perhaps in another county so that they won't feel you're in direct competition.

Check out the local zoning ordinances and licensing requirements. Network with others in home businesses, professional networking groups and associations, local Chamber of Commerce mixers, and the like. This will be invaluable for getting a feel for the market and what it takes to run a small business, for knowing what to charge for your services or product, and for avoiding the sense of isolation that can undermine your efforts. Networking is also a way to promote your business via word of mouth, thereby reducing your advertising and marketing costs.

As you begin to network, be on the lookout for someone who can serve as a mentor, someone who has gone before and who can teach you the ropes. Or you may find a group of people who act as mentors to each other. This is what happened with me. I belong to a group of writers who are in approximately the same position as I, in terms of type of work and experience level. We act as colleagues and mentors to one another. We meet periodically and call each other between meetings to get advice and feedback on a lot of nitty-gritty details—the business of being a writer. We act as each other's cheerleaders, sounding boards, advisors, and even assistant researchers. Though informal, the group has become a very important networking and support base for each of us.

Research also may include taking a course at your local community college on marketing, basic accounting and taxes, business law, and how to start a home business. SCORE, the Service Corps of Retired Executives, and the Small Business Association also offer good advice and materials for free or a nominal cost.

As you research, keep an open mind. The whole point of research is to test and refine your original idea. If your idea doesn't seem viable, don't give up completely. Analyze what the problem is and see if you can modify it in some way.

For instance, when I started freelance work, I wasn't sure whether I would be able to earn enough through writing my own articles and books. Through talking to others and other research, I concluded that indeed I could not make enough money immediately. However, rather than giving up, I explored my options. I found that by supplementing my writing with editorial work, I could not only earn what I need to earn, but I would also add some variety and new contacts to the mix. The resulting work is more satisfying than my original plan would have been.

Step Four: Garner Your Support

You will need a strong support base in order to succeed at home-based work. First and perhaps most important, you need your husband's support if you are married.

Kathleen Christensen, author of *Women and Home-Based Work: The Unspoken Contract*, discovered something interesting in her extensive survey of mothers who work from home. "When a woman made the decision to have a job at home," she says, "whether or not it worked had a lot to do with the unspoken terms of her marriage. By that I mean what a woman's implicit expectations were of herself as mother, wife, and wage earner." Christensen found that for a woman to find home-based work viable, both she and her husband had to rethink her role. If she is to add the role of wage earner to her roles of housewife and mother, then some of her work as homemaker and mother needs to be shifted to either her husband or outside help—and that has to be all right, in both their minds. "I think the most essential [step] is the psychological boundary that says 'I have work to do and I am justified in doing it.' . . . It is only when women have that kind of clarity psychologically that they will be able to get what they need," says Christensen.[4]

My own research confirms Christensen's thesis. Of the half dozen or so women I interviewed in depth, the most satisfied ones were those who had the emotional and practical support of their husbands. I talked to two women who did not have that. Their husbands (and children) resented all the long hours they put into their work and griped about the housework left undone. I couldn't help but wonder what their marriages would look like five years down the road.

Support also may mean child care. If your children are in school, you have several hours to yourself a day. Otherwise, you need to either hire some child care, or limit yourself to what you can realistically do around your youngest child's schedule. Christine Davidson, author of *Staying Home Instead: Alternatives to the Two-Paycheck Family*, suggests the following guidelines in terms of hours that can be devoted to work without child care:

Baby, birth to 4 months: Zero work; enjoy the baby and rest

Baby, 4 to 18 months: two to three hours a day

Child, 18 months to 3 years: two to four hours a day

Child, 3 to 5 years: two to four hours a day, sometimes more

School-age child: five to eight hours a day[5]

Davidson's suggestions strike me as realistic. If you find that you cannot get your work done in this amount of time, then you will have to consider finding some outside care. (In the next chapter, I give some guidelines as to how to find such care.)

Finding support also means developing a network of people who are doing something similar to what you are doing, so that you feel like you have colleagues to relate to. My writer's group serves that function for me. There is also, in my area, a support group for home-based business owners, called HENNA (Home Executives National Networking Association), which meets several times a month for mutual support.

Step Five: Set Up Your Resources

Your most important resource is you and your faith that this can work. If you take yourself seriously, other people are more likely to do so as well. You will also need persistence, because success won't happen overnight. In fact, most businesses can't expect to turn a profit within the first year. (So if you absolutely must make a certain amount of money right away, a home business may not be right at this time in your life.)

Part of thinking of and presenting yourself as a professional is having a written business plan. This describes who and where you are (name, address of business, type of ownership), what you are trying to do (goals and objectives, what service or product you are offering), and how you plan to do it (who your market is, how you plan to reach them). You should also include a list of equipment and supplies you will need to get started and how much it will cost you to get started.

Don't underestimate how much it may cost to start a home business. A professional look may mean the above equipment, good letterhead, perhaps a brochure or flyers, or even an ad painted on a vehicle. On the other hand, many businesses can be started on a shoestring. It does seem, however, that eventually all businesses get to the point where you will need to invest some capital, either in marketing, better equipment, hiring employees, moving to an outside office, or whatever. Make sure that you set aside enough of your profits to reinvest in your business. The adage, "It takes money to make money" is true. You will also need to set aside enough of your income to pay taxes. You will need to pay quarterly estimated taxes, which includes Social Security (15.3 percent) and income taxes. Failing to plan for these expenses can mean trouble when taxes are due, when machines fail, or some other necessary expense comes up.

Once your business plan and the finances are in place (or once you've convinced your employer to let you work from home), set up your work area. It's essential that you have some workspace separate from the living area. Mershon Shrigley, who has her own marketing-communications business, started at her kitchen table. She soon realized that "if I am going to do this, I must do it right." She gutted a spare bedroom and made it inviting: subdued blue-and-rose wallpaper, white furniture, rose lamps. "I tell people that if your office is in a corner of the basement, you're doomed before you start. If it's not inviting you won't want to work there."

It's ideal if you can set aside a whole room for this, but if that's not feasible, find some special place for your work station. Design the area so that you can set up and clean up quickly and keep your important equipment and papers safe from little hands.

Invest in whatever equipment you need. The minimum would be a good chair, desk, and telephone. Regarding telephones, you may need or want a separate business line, or at least call-waiting, for a professional image, and an answering machine. You will have to get stationery and business cards printed.

These are the minimum requirements. In addition, you may well need a computer, fax machine, photocopying machine, and postal scale. And, of course, if your business involves making a product, you will also need the materials.

Set up a record-keeping system that is simple yet detailed enough that at tax time you will know how much you've spent on advertising, materials, phone calls, and other business expenses, which are all tax deductible.

Step Six: Market Your Product or Service

Once you're ready to hang out your shingle, you have to let people know about your product or service. If you have done your homework in step 3, you already know what your market is. Now you have to figure out how to reach them. The three main avenues are advertising, public relations, and networking. Advertising can be done through newspaper or magazine ads (make sure it's narrowly targeted to your specific audience, or you'll waste your money), direct mail (if you have some sort of mailing list), the Yellow Pages, flyers, and word of mouth. Public relations is anything that gets your name before the public. It includes free publicity through newspapers (if you have something newsworthy, you can send a press release to the local newspapers for this kind of publicity), promotions (for example, an open house to introduce people to your business, offering free food and prizes, of course), seminars and workshops, talk shows. Finally, networking is an invaluable way to spread the news of what you're doing and learn more about your market.

If all this seems overwhelming, don't despair. It's really a matter of taking it one step at a time. Let's take a look at someone who has done just that, for a picture of how all this works out in real life.

Bette Fetter *and* Young Rembrandts

Bette Fetter is an example of someone who followed her interests and eventually saw her interests and skills coalesce into an exciting home-based business. She graduated with a degree in studio art and worked as a graphic designer, then in a number of retail managerial positions (managing a clothing store). After her first daughter, Laurie, was born, she began working part-time with a Montessori school. She immersed herself in whatever she could find pertaining to child development and began doing parenting seminars, promotional work, and "just about everything you can think of," she says. By the time she had her third child, Elizabeth, she took a couple of years to concentrate on painting, another love of hers.

During that time a friend and neighbor kept asking Bette to teach her kids how to draw. "I didn't think I knew anything about that," Bette says, "but finally for her birthday, I agreed to give her kids drawing lessons." She found she enjoyed it a lot and kept it up a couple of afternoons a week, inviting the neighborhood kids over to draw and color at the family's dining room table.

Something happened during that period. The teacher at the school Elizabeth attended came over one day and saw what the children were drawing. She was impressed. "Other kids this age don't draw like this," she told Bette. "You have something special here." The woman asked Bette if she would be willing to offer her drawing classes at the school as well.

Bette didn't think parents would be interested in signing their preschoolers up for drawing class, but her husband, Bill, suggested she try it out anyway. "You never know where it might lead," he told her. She went to the school, and within a couple of days fourteen children were signed up for the class. She taught classes there one afternoon a week, continually perfecting the teaching method and curriculum.

As parents saw the dramatic results in their children's art work, news spread of Bette's unique curriculum. "It's unlike any other way people teach children to draw," she says. "My approach came from working with kids and observing them, learning how their minds worked, and introducing art in ways they can understand and respond to." She points to several "before" and "after" pictures children have drawn. The differences are dramatic—what you'd expect after several weeks of lessons. However, in this case only one lesson made the difference.

And so *Young Rembrandts* was born. Word spread concerning Bette's program, and more and more schools, day care centers, and park districts asked for her services. Her business was growing. Things got hectic at home. Her husband, Bill, had been climbing the corporate ladder in sales and wasn't home as much as either of them would like. "There was all this life stuff to handle," as well as the work load, Bette said. "One day I realized that I was getting four kids ready for school every morning, while Bill just had to get himself to work. That wasn't right." She and Bill sat down and renegotiated how things would be done around the house, so that she could have the time to get everything done. Bill had always done all the laundry; now he added getting the kids ready for school. "We just made a list and divided things up, according to what would be the easiest for each of us to do," Bill says.

As more and more and more opportunities for *Young Rembrandts* opened up, Bill began to envision its potential. One day he said to Bette, "I know what I want to do next. I want to work with you on *Rembrandts*." Bette's first reaction was, "Get real," but the more she thought about it, the more it made sense. There were obvious limitations to what she could do. She was still a mom with four children, and her family always came first. Bill had a lot of wonderful business knowledge that would complement her own experience. Yes, they decided, it would make a lot of sense. So for the next eight months, they strategically planned how to grow the business to the point where Bill could quit his sales job and come home to work.

They both thrive on the flexibility of working from home together. They keep regular hours, working in the office from 8:30 until 1:15, when one of them picks up Matthew, age four, from his preschool. Then the older kids are home from school, and the afternoons and much of the evenings are devoted to "life stuff." After the kids are in bed, one or both of them may work a couple of hours in the office again, but they try not to let the business take over the family.

Bette and Bill have found a situation that allows them to perfectly express their design. Bette's key energized ability is creating, and everything she does is related to creating. Art is obviously creative; so is child rearing. She also sees herself as creating a business. Relationships are also important to both her and Bill. Bill's key energized outcome is to "make a difference in the lives of others." As he puts it, "I think if you're put on this planet, you have a responsibility to make it better in some way." In his work with *Young Rembrandts*, as a parent, and as a soccer coach, his concern is to help young people achieve their potential and express all their gifts. It excites him to see how children's confidence and ability to express themselves grows when they just learn a new technique, whether it's in art or soccer.

As Perceivers, the Fetters enjoy the way family and work flow into each other and enrich each other. "I'll be on the phone, talking about liability insurance with my insurance agent," Bill says, "and as soon as I get off, my four-year-old asks me, 'How do they make concrete?' What's the more challenging question here—liability insurance or how concrete is made!"

Bill and Bette also find their skills and interests are complementary. She develops the curriculum and trains the teachers, he does a lot on the business side (marketing, contracts, hiring). He's also the visionary of where the business can go. She says, "I'm on the mom-and-pop level with people, but Bill's view is national. He keeps throwing out the anchor point and making me broaden my viewpoint."

Bette's home business flowed from her loves (children and art), her background (everything she had done beforehand—from management, to giving seminars, to child development—taught her skills she uses in *Young Rembrandts*), and her personal style. Though she still has limits to how many hours she will work right now, she looks ahead to when her children don't need her. By then, she should have a thriving business, working with her husband in a very satisfactory arrangement.

As Bette demonstrates, it is possible to find your own

way to work from home successfully. But there are always trade-offs. Some of the pitfalls, however, are avoidable.

Pitfalls to Avoid

"The thing I like most about working from home is that I can eat whenever I want," Charlene said. "The thing I like least about it is that I can eat whenever I want." Charlene's remark points out the double-edged nature of working from home: The very advantages can also squirm into disadvantages. The downside of flexibility is that it's hard to separate work from family. The dark side of having total control is that you alone are responsible for getting yourself motivated.

Traditionally, the home has been seen as a private place, the place you go to get away from work pressures. Combining the two "worlds" of work and home presents some unique challenges. What are some of the pitfalls Bette and other women who have made a success of working from home have managed to work out, and how did they do so?

Not being taken seriously. If you leave an office situation to do your work at home, your colleagues or employer may assume you're less committed. If you start a home business, others may think you're "just doing a little something on the side for pin money." The way to dispel such notions is to take yourself seriously, project a professional image, and prove by the excellence of your work that you are truly a professional.

Lack of support. There will always be people who will tell you why something can't be done. I like what the Fetters do about such people. They started a "No Vision" file. In it are the names and addresses of everyone who said nobody would be interested in their idea (including some bankers who refused to lend them money). "Someday," Bette says, "we're going to send those people press clippings, bank statements, and our income tax records to show how wrong they were!"

Obviously, if someone who genuinely cares about you

expresses a reservation about your enterprise, you would do well to hear them out. They may see something important you've missed. But you don't need people who are just bent on thwarting you. Surround yourself with positive people who believe in you, and let the naysayers drift to the edges of your life if you can. You're going to be too busy proving them wrong to waste time and energy fighting their negativity.

Separating work from family life. It is necessary to set boundaries between work and family or you'll be burdened by constant guilt. Even the Fetters, who enjoyed the fluid lines between work and family life, found it necessary to set boundaries. I and others have found that setting up a schedule and sticking to it, finding the right place for an office, using an answering machine, arranging for child care, all help. Other tactics people find helpful are: setting a ritual for starting and stopping work (such as going out to get the paper and coming back in to start work), packing up work at the end of the day, and not answering the doorbell or personal calls during work hours. You may also find it hard to keep from throwing in a load of laundry or letting other household tasks distract you. I play a little mental game with myself: I remind myself that if I were away at my office, I wouldn't be doing those things, so why should I do them now? I felt very empowered once when I sat in my office while someone rang and rang my doorbell. I decided that while I was working, I would treat it exactly as if I were away at another location.

Loneliness and isolation. Even if you see people every day outside your work responsibilities, it can still feel lonely working from home. Here is where it's so helpful to have a network of "colleagues"—other women who are working from home, preferably in your field or something like it. I call my writer friends often during the week. Even if I get their answering machine, I feel somehow less lonely; I imagine they are really there, working on some deadline, and not answering their phone. I know I will hear from them shortly.

Interruptions. The same methods that will help you keep family and work separate will also tend to cut down on interruptions. The trick is to be self-disciplined about it. I find that when I tell people this is not a good time for me, they usually respect it. Interruptions from family members are harder to handle. Sometimes you just have to flex, other times you need to firmly remind them that this is your work time.

Housework doesn't get done. Reexamine your and your husband's expectations of your role. It's unreasonable to expect you to be able to work and take care of all the household and child care responsibilities as if you did not have a job. Either renegotiate the division of labor, hire extra household help or child care, or revise your expectations of how much will get done. Remind your husband (and yourself!) that just because you are home all day doesn't mean that you have all day to take care of the house.

Trouble getting motivated. Keeping to a schedule helps here. It also helps to know when you have the most and the least energy throughout the day. Schedule your most challenging work during your "peak" times, the more routine stuff when your energy is lower. If motivation is a chronic problem, there's probably something about the job or the work setup that is going against your design. Try to figure out what it is, correct it if you can, or change course completely and find something else to do.

At some point, you may find your home-based business grows to the point where the work requires someone full-time. At that point, your options are to either hire someone to take up the slack, or expand your hours. In the next chapter, we'll look at some of the dynamics of working full-time. A full-time home-based business has one distinct advantage: You are in control, you possess the one ingredient that makes combining full-time work and family doable—flexibility.

CHAPTER TEN
WORKING FULL-TIME

I have a dream. In my vision of the ideal workplace, people who want to either take time out or reduce their hours for family or personal reasons would be allowed to do so without penalty to their careers. Their dedication to raising the future generation, or for finding balance in their lives, would be seen as laudable. What they would bring back to the workplace, should they choose to come back full-time, would be recognized as valuable experience and taken into account as part of their qualifications. The opportunities would be there for women who do want to devote themselves primarily to career, but the system would not penalize those who do not or cannot.

That is my dream. The reality is that, while there are some gains toward flexibility being made in some industries, most companies measure productivity in terms of "face time"—time spent in the office. The "old male norm" is still very much in effect in the workplace.

> The profound reality is that the workplace was designed over time not for women with family responsibilities, not for two-job households, not for women whose skills were honed running a home rather than a corporation. The workplace was designed and evolved over time for men who lived in two-parent households, in which the division of labor was quite clear: The private sphere of the

home was the woman's responsibility; the public sphere
of breadwinning was the man's.[1]

This means that many women who work full-time will
feel conflicted over work and family: single mothers, women
whose husbands don't earn enough to support even a modest
standard of living, women who for one reason or another have
to work to pay off debt. It also means that women who enjoy
or choose to work full-time may also feel squeezed as far as
not having much of a personal life. One single young woman
said, "Because I'm single, I'm expected to socialize with
people from work after hours. I want to date, to go to school
perhaps—I want to have some kind of personal life outside the
job. But in my field [marketing], it's so competitive that I'm
afraid if I do back off from some of these things, I'll damage
myself professionally."

A recent poll of 3,400 workers, conducted by the
Families and Work Institute of New York, found that
Americans believe they are working more hours: Forty-three
percent said the demands of their jobs are "excessive," and
twenty-four percent said they had "no time for family." Nearly
half of these stressed-out workers are women, many of them
mothers who struggle not only with the longer hours and
extra work at the office but also with an equally demanding
family life.[2]

Not all women, or even all mothers, who work full-time
feel stressed, however. Faye Crosby, author of *Juggling*, cites
several studies that seem to suggest that juggling multiple
roles increases a woman's resistance to depression—but only
when roles contain enough reward.[3]

Some women find fulfillment and satisfaction in the very
act of balancing career and home, or home and volunteer
work, or home and a significant commitment to some cause,
or . . . the list is almost endless.

If some women handle the juggling act well while others

don't, what is the difference between these two groups? Studies suggest several factors. According to Crosby, "Several psychologists have documented, in different locations and with different samples, that a woman's mental health depends on the nature of her job, her closeness to her husband, and the tasks she faces as a mother."[4] In other words, if she is supported in what she does by her husband, if she feels good about herself as a mother, and if her job fits her and complements her mothering, she is likely to find satisfaction in juggling her multiple roles.

But there's another crucial factor that applies to every woman with children at home: child care. One study showed that adequate child care is the single most important factor for relieving role strain with working mothers.[5]

Let's look at each of these factors in turn. If you're considering working full-time, you can gauge how well your resources match the demands of this lifestyle and anticipate probable stress points. If you're already working full-time and feeling stressed, this list may help you pinpoint exactly where the problems lie. Then we'll look at some ways to alleviate the most common stresses.

Support from Your Husband

Without support from your husband, you may find yourself working "the second shift": a full-time job for pay, plus a full-time job working within the family. This is not only unfair, it is nearly impossible for anyone but the most energetic of women.

The traditional model is that the husband is the breadwinner, the wife takes care of the domestic front. The implicit understanding underlying this is that each of these is a very demanding role. If the wife, out of necessity or election, takes on the "male role" (in an environment that demands her best energies and much of her time), then she must decrease the time and energy spent in the domestic sphere. That may mean sharing the domestic chores with her husband and children, not doing some things, and/or buying goods and services she can no longer supply with her own labor.

Most men who want their wives to work see the logic in this—or can be made to see the logic! All of the women I interviewed who have any kind of paying job and were happy with it said they had the support of their husbands. Those who were not happy or who were very stressed had husbands who expected them to be both traditional wives *and* breadwinners.

So what do you do if your husband is in this category? What if he doesn't support your working?

First of all, I suggest you sit down and talk through your reasons for working. If he doesn't agree with them, that is an important issue for you to settle before you do anything else. I do not believe God will bless your efforts if you go against your husband's wishes on this major area.

More often, the husband agrees in theory with the necessity to work full-time, but he doesn't want to make any changes. In that case, you need to discuss all the things that need to be done around the house. Make a list. Talk it through: Since you no longer will have as many hours to do these things as you once had, how will they get done? If you can't afford to hire out some services, what will you let go and what will you divide up? If your children are old enough, this would be a great way to teach them some more responsibility. But do it as a family: Sit down and talk through the options and divide up the chores among everyone.

A crucial step here, according to one woman I talked to, is to let your husband or children take full responsibility. If your husband takes over the laundry and he doesn't do it, it won't get done. Don't you end up doing things left undone, or you will just be putting yourself into superwoman mode and the family's expectations will follow.

Knowing your design, and having an idea of your husband's and children's dislikes, should help in this division of labor, by the way. As much as possible, go with the strengths and preferences of each person and divide up the chores no one wants on a rotating basis.

Feeling Good About Your Mothering

In chapter 6 we discussed how your design affects your mothering style. Basing your mothering style around your strengths and setting realistic goals for areas that are not strengths can certainly improve how you feel about yourself as a mother—which should also go a long way toward alleviating some of your role stress.

One thing most mothers feel, whether they work for pay or not, is guilt. But mothers who are employed full-time usually experience extra guilt. Sometimes it is true guilt—we really may be out of balance. Maryann was working four mornings a week and several nights. Her husband worked a full-time job and was also a musician, which meant he was gone many evenings and weekends. During one particularly stressful period when both Maryann and her husband were working many hours, they got a call from their son's teacher. At first Maryann felt very guilty about what the teacher reported; it was obvious that her son was showing signs of stress. But she used her guilt to make some changes. She realized that her night job was too much, and she quit. In that case, guilt was productive: Maryann could change the situation, and she did.

But sometimes the guilt is false guilt, a result of "shoulds" that we take upon ourselves that God does not require of us. I like what Miriam Neff suggests in her book, *Working Moms*, to help us distinguish between true and false guilt: Ask yourself the question, "Whom am I trying to please and why?" When you recognize true guilt, do something about it, as Maryann did. If you are truly trying to please the Lord, if you are honestly taking into account the needs of your family and you have explored all your options and chosen the best option for you and your family, then dismiss the guilt as false guilt. Trust that God's grace will cover any lacks.

The Nature of Your Job

Your job itself, of course, contributes largely to your satisfaction or dissatisfaction with working full-time. The moms I talked to who had paying jobs, especially those who work full-time, said that they have no "me time." If the job is satisfying, it can serve as "me time," a way to find balance for yourself and to express yourself. If the job is not satisfying, you're more likely to feel frustrated by always having to do for others and never having time for yourself.

Since you have some idea of your design already, you have a distinct advantage at least in knowing what kind of work would be satisfying. You may have to settle for finding one or two of your key design elements in your job, but do try your best to find satisfying work. If you want more help in the career-related parts of your design, I suggest you look into the materials mentioned in the Resources.

No job is perfect; there will always be tradeoffs. But when you're working full-time and trying to balance other responsibilities as well, you need to step back and take a look at the overall balance. You may find that you're using your energized skills in your job, but you still come home feeling too drained. This happened to Joan, a social worker with two young girls. When she was working as an outpatient therapist for children and families, she found that she was giving the same energies in her job as she did in her parenting: nurturing, listening, guiding, and the like. Also, she had to work many evening hours, which ate into her family time. When she was home, she felt "nurtured out." Her family was getting the leftovers, in terms of both time and energy.

Once Joan realized what the problem was, she was able to switch to working with geriatric patients in a hospital setting (which means mostly daytime hours). Though the job itself isn't as fulfilling as her former position, the tasks and the hours better complement her mothering at this time in her life.

Mary Beth is a writer who freelances from home but works full-time hours. She finds that her job complements her life, and vice versa: "I'll be on an outing with my children and come across an interesting idea for a story. My life feeds my work. If I weren't writing for money, I'd be writing for myself, because I love it. So why not do it for money?" Mary Beth doesn't feel drained by her work but energized by it.

If your job drains you more than energizes you, ask yourself why. Is it because there's no flexibility? (We'll look at some ways to deal with this later.) Is it that the job doesn't use your best skills? If so, is there any way you can rearrange your responsibilities so that you major in what you enjoy doing and can delegate the less interesting aspects of your work? Is it the sheer number of hours you work, or the responsibility you carry? Is there any way to cut back? Analyze what isn't working for you and explore alternatives.

How to Gain More Flexibility

Flexibility is the most prized aspect of a full-time job when you are also trying to balance family demands. Some of the flexible arrangements some employers use are: flextime, which allows employees to set alternative start and finish times to the work day; flexplace (telecommuting), which means employees can work off-site, either at home or from a satellite office, during all or part of their scheduled hours (usually works best if the work can be done via computer, fax machine, and/or telephone); compressed work week, in which the week's hours are worked in fewer than five days; and V-time (voluntary reduced work time), which allows full-time employers to reduce work hours for a specified period of time with a corresponding reduction in compensation. V-time is different from regular part-time work in that there is usually a time limit and the expectation that the employee will return to full-time status.[6]

Flextime and flexplace can be one way to avoid the whole latchkey-child syndrome. This is especially important because at least one study showed that twelve- and thirteen-year-olds who were latchkey kids, taking care of themselves eleven or more hours a week, were about twice as likely than supervised children to smoke, drink alcohol, and use marijuana.[7] As several mothers of teenagers told me, the need to "be there" doesn't end just because the children are growing up. In fact, several mothers I know actually cut back their hours during this stressful time because of their children's greater needs.

Flextime may offer just what's needed to combat the latchkey problem. For instance, one mother of two school-age children works from 9:00 A.M. to 3:00 P.M. two days a week and returns home to watch her children along with a neighbor's. The other three days she works from 9:00 A.M. until 6:30 P.M., when the neighbor takes over the after-school duties. She is also able to start work earlier or leave later occasionally in order to volunteer at school or take a child to a doctor appointment.

"Flextime is gaining acceptance in the workplace," says Marcia Brumit Kropf, director of research at Catalyst, a New York City-based research and advocacy group for women in business. "Five years ago, the companies we surveyed tended to offer this option on an individual basis. But today more firms are making it available as a matter of policy. Employers have realized how important it is to their workforce."[8]

According to the Work and Families Institute, flextime and flexplace seem to be the most prevalent forms of flexible options. Nationally, seventy-seven percent of Fortune 1000 companies offer some form of flextime; between twenty-nine and forty-four percent of employees in the Families and Work Institute study worked for companies that allow some sort of flexibility in terms of start and end times or extended lunch breaks. Twenty-four percent of American employees work for companies that allow them to work at home regularly, and thirty-five percent of Fortune 1000 companies offer at least some of their employees the option to telecommute. The other options are less widely available.

If your company does not currently offer some kind of flexible arrangement, you may be able to persuade them. But do your homework first. Write to the Families and Work Institute or the U.S. Department of Labor for free information on how companies can choose, use, and implement flexible options.[9] Call the personnel department of companies similar to your own for their policies and how they are working out. Ask co-workers what schedules would work best for them and what they would need in terms of staffing. Highlight the benefits to your employer, based on your research, and answer any objections that may come up. For instance, by allowing workers to come in earlier or stay later, they may save on overtime and make it easier for employees to service clients in different time zones.

Propose a pilot program, perhaps on one department (yours, of course!) on a trial basis. Needless to say, you have to do your part then to show how this option makes you a *more* motivated, *more* responsible, *more* productive employee. Work extra hard to communicate with co-workers and your supervisor and to be there during critical staffing times.

With flexibility in their job, many women who are employed full-time find they can still balance family and job fairly well. However, one important aspect must also be in place for all who work when their child is not in school: good child care.

Find Good Child Care

My own informal research confirms what academic studies have found: Child care can be the deciding factor in whether a mother is able to make peace with working full-time or not. Those who felt good about their child's caregivers were able to concentrate on and enjoy their jobs. Those who experienced problems in this area endured great stress.

Some fortunate women have relatives who are willing and able to take care of their children. One mom I know who works from home full-time has her mother living with her and taking care of her children. Another woman who works irregular and fluctuating hours has a sister take care of her children.

For those of us who are not near relatives who are able to care for our children, finding good child care is a matter of networking with other moms and organizations. Churches, neighbors, and baby-sitting co-ops are other avenues to check out. Depending on the ages of your children, you may find that an in-home caregiver, family day care, a day care center, a preschool, or an after-school program will fit your needs. If you can take advantage of flextime and/or flexplace, you may find another mom who does the same thing with whom you can swap child care. Especially if you both have only one child to care for during these hours, this can be a good arrangement.

Finding good care means knowing your child and finding the best option to fit. Does your child seem to welcome new experiences and relish being with other children? That will make a difference in what you choose; he or she may find a center stimulating. On the other hand, is your child more timid, quiet—someone who enjoys playing by himself? Then you may want to concentrate on finding the best family situation you can, where your child will deal with a smaller number of other children.

In her book, *Working Moms*, Miriam Neff offers the following guidelines for looking for child care:[10]

1. *Allow yourself plenty of time.* I know from personal experience that there is nothing worse than rushing into a decision. I suggest you find both your primary caregiver and

a good backup. In one case, my backup became my next caregiver when I grew dissatisfied with the first one.

2. *Focus on* who *rather than* what. You will obviously want a safe, clean place with adequate equipment, but the person who takes care of your child is more important than the program.

3. *Spend time observing before you make your decision.* Angela Edwards, a teacher and child development expert, suggests going to the place, finding an unobtrusive corner, closing your eyes, and *listening.* "If you hear children singing, sign on the dotted line right away." The reason? Happy children, relaxed children, will sing, Edwards says. Also listen for the tone of voice children use with each other, and the caregiver uses with the children. Now open your eyes. Look at the children's faces. Are they happy? Are the children busy or bored? What happens when something goes wrong? How does the caregiver handle it? Try to imagine how you would feel if you had to be there eight to ten hours a day.

4. *Find out the turnover rate.* If you're considering a center, ask about the turnover rate for teachers and aides, Neff advises. Find out how much they're paid. These are indicators of quality of care.

If you're considering a nanny or family day-care provider, find out how long she has been doing this and ask how long she intends to do daycare. Also ask how often she or her children, if she has any, have gotten sick. You need reliable care. My current caregiver has been providing family day care for over ten years and is never sick. She is most reliable and obviously content with her job.

5. *Once you've made the decision, stay involved.* "Keep communication open and frequent," Neff advises. "Your child can't express all that occurs. Monitor, ask, observe. Establish a positive working relationship with the staff. The hours of your child's day are dependent on it."

I have found from personal experience and the interviews I've done, that a good caregiver can enhance your child's life. "I never felt I had to settle for second-best for a caregiver," said Joan, the social worker with two children. "I just looked and looked until I was satisfied, and then I monitored what was going on. I think if a child is traumatized by leaving a parent, something is wrong. It could be that the parent is communicating they are not confident about the caregiver, or about working and leaving the child. Or they come back, and they are very harried."

As a social worker, Joan did extensive personal research on the effects of other-than-mother care on children. The research is often contradictory, but what stands out is that if a mother is comfortable with her decision and has chosen a good caregiver she is comfortable with, the child will most likely be fine. In fact, some studies show that children of employed parents are often more intellectually developed than children whose mothers were not employed.

I've already discussed the timing of working in terms of children's needs, in chapter 7. The bottom line keeps coming down to this: You need to decide with your husband before God (if you're married), what is best for your family, with its unique constellation of needs and gifts and resources. I only offer this counsel: Pray constantly for wisdom, be tuned in to your children's needs and experiences, and be ready to change as your family's needs change.

Managing the Juggling Act

Even if you can take advantage of flextime, flexplace, or even part-time options, balancing family and work responsibilities is a juggling act, especially if the children are still young. Once they are in school, you're also juggling their after-school activities. What does it take to manage this well?

Look at the following list and see how well it matches up with your resources and elements of your design.

Organizational ability. No doubt about it, those women who are successfully combining work and mothering have learned to be more organized. Louise, who has a five-year-old and an infant and works three days a week, plans out every detail of her week on Sunday. She even knows exactly what she and the children will wear on Thursday! (No doubt Louise is a Judger and probably also prefers Thinking and Sensing.)

Those of us with fewer natural organizational skills have two options: Learn to become more organized, or learn to live with some things undone. I myself am working on both.

Resources to hire help. Another common strategy for anyone who was able to afford it was to hire someone to clean house twice a month. Most of the women who were employed in any way said they do this. If this is at all possible for you financially, I advise it. Even a teenager may be trained to do a passable job, cleaning house.

Realistic expectations. We have to reassess our expectations of ourselves and our role. Sometimes it is difficult to let go of the old expectations that were bred into us. Many of us were raised by mothers who did not work outside the home. We may have nevertheless internalized the picture of Mom at home, baking cookies, cleaning, being always available to take the children to the park and to cook sumptuous meals for the husband. If we did take time out to do these things, both we and our families may expect it to continue. Then, when we enter the workplace, we simply add on to our identity another role, that of "worker," but we don't revise our expectations of what it means to be Mom. We try to be two people at once, and we feel guilty when we can't "bring home the bacon and fry it up too."

But working full-time means less time to do other things. We have to find ways to major on the important things and let go of the less important. There needs to be a shift in our thinking of how the family is run. This will probably include dividing up chores as a family—and doing chores together, making simpler meals, hiring help, or going without some things getting done (like washing windows).

Creative ways for personal and spouse time. The women I interviewed also were candid about what gets neglected: "me time" and "husband time." "My 'me time' is the time I spend working," said one woman. This is why I keep stressing how important it is to express some aspects of your design in both your work and family life. If one or the other, or both, draws on your key motivations, then you will be likely to feel some satisfaction even in the midst of your juggling act.

I'm disturbed by the prevalence of sacrificing "husband time." One single mom I know attributes her divorce to the way she and her husband concentrated all their energy on the children and neglected the marriage. Another woman, a new empty nester, stressed how important it is not to neglect that relationship while the children are young. I agree.

Make time, at least once a week, when just you and your spouse can talk about other things besides the children. Many couples hire a baby-sitter and go out. Even if you can't do that, set aside one evening a week when you and your husband will get together over coffee and dessert after the children are in bed. The ground rule is: Don't talk about the kids but about your own lives. Another option that would allow you to get out is to swap baby-sitting with another couple once or twice a month. You can go out to a cheap movie and for dessert, or even just dessert. One couple I know had a standing date to go out for breakfast (which is cheaper than lunch or dinner) every Saturday.

A close network with other parents. You will come to depend on other parents for carpooling, back-up child care, emergencies, information on what to do when your child gets chicken pox, and a myriad of other daily survival issues. It's also good to know the parents of your children's friends, so you know who is influencing them.

A strong spiritual life. The greatest resource you have will be your own relationship with God, fostered through prayer and personal Bible study. Remember Jesus' words, which every working mother can take to heart: "Come to me, all you who are weary and burdened, and I will give you rest. Take my yoke upon you and learn from me, for I am gentle and humble in heart, and you will find rest for your souls. For my yoke is easy and my burden light" (Matt. 11:28–30).

When you need strength for the day after a sleepless night with a sick child, prayer is your source of that strength. When you are weary with the daily schedules and constant juggling, come to Jesus for rest. When you need wisdom for the myriad difficult decisions that will face you, you can go to God (James 1:5). When guilt descends, you can pray about whether it's true or false guilt; you can be forgiven; you can find direction; you can move on. Jill Briscoe said, "If Jesus is first, you'll know what to do next." You are seeking to serve him with your gifts in family and the world; don't lose sight of that. Someday, I believe, he will also say to you, "Well done, good and faithful servant! . . . Come and share your master's happiness!" (Matt. 25:21).

CHAPTER ELEVEN
TAKING CHARGE
OF YOUR LIFE

$\mathcal{I}$ have long been fascinated by people who are successful—not successful in worldly terms but successful in terms of living lives that are productive, lives that make a difference in the world somehow, lives that are obviously deeply satisfying to themselves.

Several of the women I interviewed for this book fit this category. There is Mary Beth Sammons, the writer and mother of three children, Caitlin, nine, Thomas, six, and Emily, eighteen months. Mary Beth's life is strenuous. She is up at 5:30 A.M., does her housework and gets the older two children off to school by 8:30. Then, if it's one of the two days her baby goes to day care, she will sit down to her computer and "power work" to finish her writing assignments. Mary Beth is a regular freelancer for the *Chicago Tribune*, a stringer for *Family Circle* magazine, and a regular freelancer for several other magazines. Writing is a key element of her design, but she has honed it to fit in with her energized outcome and life purpose: to inspire people to do good. "I was looking for ways to help in the community," she says. "I did some volunteer work, but then my boss said something to me that changed my focus. She said, 'You can go help in a soup kitchen and try to do the work of ten people, or you can write about the soup kitchen and inspire ten people to go out and help.' That made me realize that I can be a mom and take my gifts and use them in a way that can help other people."

Mary Beth is living a life she loves, despite the many tradeoffs. She spends both quality and quantity time with her children, she knows her life purpose, and she is using her gifts in living out her purpose.

In studying the lives of women who have found some kind of balance, who find satisfaction in their lives, I have discovered that these women share some common characteristics. First, they have discovered who they are. By accident or by careful thought, they have gotten in touch with what they love to do. Second, they have focused their deepest values enough to have some sense of their life purpose.

In this book I have attempted to give you tools for discovering and developing these first two elements. The third characteristic of successful, balanced women is that they take responsibility for their lives. Rather than let circumstances shape them, they decide to shape the circumstances of their lives according to their design and their purpose.

In the process of doing this, they also develop some other life skills that make them effective, no matter what "season" of life they are in. I want to turn now to what these skills are. Honing these skills will serve you well all the days of your life.

Life Skill #1: Trust in God

Perhaps it's unusual to think of trust in God as a *skill*. And yet trusting God is something we grow better at doing, the more we do it. As we trust him in the little things, we grow in our ability to trust in the larger things. And it is something we consciously decide to do (or not do).

Trust in God is so important because there will be times in everyone's life where it seems impossible to "design a life of one's own." There are times when we will have to postpone our own needs for satisfying work because of more pressing needs. After Deana's husband left her and her young son, her main goal was survival, emotional and financial. She took the first job she could find that would provide her some flexibility and the income she needed. However, after several years spent in healing, she now feels ready to look for more satisfying work.

Maryann consciously set aside her desire for a life that could fit her to help launch her husband's music career. She and her husband have two preschool children; she works part-time while he works a full-time job to pay the bills and nurtures his growing musical career. Life is hard for her now, but she is finding ways to use a few of her energized abilities and trusting God for a time when it will be "her turn" to find work that fits her.

Maryann illustrates that even during those times when our situation is not what we would want it, a knowledge of our design can help us cope more effectively with our situation.

Trust in God at such times means believing he has his hand in our lives even when things are difficult. It means leaning into difficulty to learn what we can of God and ourselves. It means seeking opportunities to use our gifts, believing that eventually he will provide a way.

Life Skill #2: Decision Making

I wish someone had taught me the process of making really sound decisions before I made lots of the big ones! However, I have learned some things along the way that have helped me make better decisions . . . decisions about finances, about life direction, about work issues.

Step One: Pray. This is not just a pat suggestion. I believe that it truly is the foundation for everything that follows in the process. I pray that God will help me see all the facts, that he will help me anticipate consequences, that he will help me understand how a decision will affect myself and others. I pray he will help me know when to actually make the decision. (Remember, I'm a Perceiver who prefers to gather data forever rather than come to a decision. A Judger may need to pray that she doesn't come to closure too soon.) I pray that God would speak to me through his Word, through the insights of others, and through my own inner convictions.

Step Two: Clarify the problem or your objective. This may seem obvious, but too often people jump right into comparing options without ever really clarifying what they want.

For instance, I was frustrated about the seeming lack of space in our house. The apparent answer was to move into a larger home, but since that would have meant added expense and the hassle of moving, I decided to think through what I really wanted. I realized that what I wanted was a clutter-free house and home office. Once I clarified the real problem and my objective, other solutions besides moving came to mind. I am now working on getting more organized and investigating space-saving ideas. If I had not taken the trouble to clarify what I really wanted, I may have chosen the most obvious solution, which isn't always the best.

Step Three: Study the situation or problem. This is basically a Sensing step, in Myers-Briggs terms. Isabel Myers suggests asking questions such as:

What are the facts?
What exactly is the situation?
What has been done?
What has worked?
What are the bottom-line realities?
What are my resources?[1]

If Sensing is not your preference, it may be wise to sit down and work through this with someone who is good at looking at the realities. In fact, seeking the input of people you trust, especially if their gifts differ from yours, is wise to do throughout the decision-making process.

Step Four: Generate options. This is an Intuitive step, in which you consider all the possibilities. Brainstorm all options (better yet, get an Intuitive to brainstorm with you). Don't leave anything out just because it seems impractical; sometimes the impractical ideas contain the germ of a creative solution.

After you've brainstormed all the options, come up with several (at least three) potentially viable solutions or alternatives.

Step Five: Compare each alternative with your objective. Before you compare alternatives with each other and look at the potential consequences, compare it with your original objective. You might find that Alternative A doesn't meet the objective at all. You'll save yourself time and energy by not including it in the next steps.

Step Six: Weigh the consequences of each alternative. Objectively look at the advantages and disadvantages. Some questions to ask might be:

What are the pros and cons of each alternative?
What are the logical consequences of each?
Is this reasonable?
What are the consequences of not acting?
What impact would this have on my other priorities?[2]
Does this violate God's moral law in any way?

Step Seven: Look at the impact on people. Now you are using feeling-judgment to put yourself into the situation empathetically and consider the impact of each option in personal terms. Some questions to consider:

How does each alternative fit with my values?
How will the people concerned be affected?
How will each option contribute to harmony?
How will I support people with this decision?[3]
Does this allow me to contribute in some way to the needs
   of people?

Step Eight: Choose the best option. Some decisions may be weighted by logic or by values. When deciding about leaving my job once I had my baby, I put more weight on feeling-judgment criteria. When I realized I was overcommitted, I gave more weight to the logical criteria; all my commitments fit with my values, but spreading myself too thin was undermining my effectiveness.

Step Nine: Act on your choice. Trust that God will be with you and will lead you to a course correction if needed.

Step Ten: Keep praying, and evaluate. It's helpful to keep an open mind. Perhaps you did not consider all the facts, possibilities, consequences, or impacts. You may have new information that casts everything in a different light. The situation may change, or you may change, or you might run into unforeseen consequences. Don't be afraid to change your mind or your direction.

Life Skill #3: Risk-Taking

I'm convinced that anyone who wants to design a life she can love for herself must be willing to take risks. No matter which choice we make, there will be people who don't support it. There will be roadblocks to overcome. Staying home with children opens you up to ridicule from people who believe you're "wasting your mind" or education; choosing to work outside the home puts you at risk for being judged by others as an uncaring mother. Choosing not to have children risks the judgment of "selfishness"; choosing not to marry risks being labeled as odd.

Even discovering your design opens you to the risk of needing to change some things in your life, and change is never easy. But choose we must, because we are responsible to God for the stewardship of the gifts and the circumstances of our lives.

The willingness to take risks leads us to "Experience Doing," one of the "critical career competencies" Adele

Scheele has isolated from the lives of successful people. When we Experience Doing, we act, we experiment, we try new things and try on new behaviors, we express our opinions, and we "create occasions for developing and exhibiting skills that had not otherwise been available to us."[4] All your Satisfying Activities were examples of Experiencing Doing. As you build on these, and as you try new things, you increase both your competence and confidence. You begin to develop the mind-set that you can make things happen for yourself; you do not have to let life happen to you. You take responsibility for your life. You grow up.

Risk is involved in all the life skills mentioned. Whenever you connect with someone, whenever you offer your skills to the world, you risk rejection or misunderstanding. Whenever you attempt something you've never done before, you risk failure.

But *risk* is really another word for faith. I've always been struck in the parable of the talents by the attitude of the man who had received one talent. First of all, he had a wrong view of the master: "'Master,'" he said, "'I knew that you are a hard man, harvesting where you have not sown and gathering where you have not scattered seed.'" Second, he was afraid to take any risks: "'I was afraid and went out and hid your talent in the ground'" (Matt. 25:24–25). We are called to invest our lives and our gifts for God. Those who are too afraid to do so merely exchange one risk for another: They risk having even what they've been given taken away (Matt. 25:29).

Life Skill #4: Connecting

Women's lives traditionally have centered around the connections we are able to make. However, while we have been good at making connections in our personal lives, studies show that women do not "network"as proficiently as men in their work lives.[5] And I'm concerned that in our busyness, we are doing less connecting even in our personal lives.

Networking, or connecting with people, is essential for our own mental health. Some studies suggest that women who are not employed outside the home are more prone to depression. However, I would want to know the conditions that lead to depression. Surely it's not staying home per se but the isolation that often happens when women at home with young children do not know anyone else in the same situation. Having an outside job may provide what Faye Crosby calls "amplification": You have more people to tell the good things to, more people who will be your audience and give you feedback, and more potential for a variety of positive responses. This is important for all of us, no matter what our life situation.

Connecting is important for finding jobs, for creating new options for ourselves. People have to know who we are, what we have to offer. Overwhelmingly, the best jobs are found through personal contacts—though not necessarily through the people we know well. The best contacts are what Wayne E. Baker calls "weak contacts"—old contacts left dormant for years, an acquaintance at a previous employer, a former neighbor, a friend of a friend. The reason is they are "bridges" to new information. Those with whom you have strong ties probably know the same people, information, and job leads that you do. But those with whom you have weak ties are privy to information about job openings and opportunities you don't know about.

I've seen this work out in my own life, time and time again. In researching this book, for instance, I came across a number of fascinating women. As I discussed my interests and concerns with them, each one told me of someone she knew who was doing something interesting or knew something I needed to know. In some cases, new opportunities opened up for me as I linked up with others who share my interests. This is how we generate new opportunities for ourselves.

I suggest that you develop at least three kinds of connections or networks, no matter what your situation.

1. *Peers.* This should be your widest network. Peers are people with whom you share something in common. They validate your choices because they have made the same choices. They help you problem-solve because they are in the same situation.

If you are a mother at home, you need a network of other moms to relate to. If you're single, you need others who share your concerns and can provide companionship. If you're employed, seek others at work and at church who share your struggles and interests. If there's a problem you're struggling with, such as a child with Attention Deficit Disorder, seek a support group of other parents struggling with the same problem.

If peers are not apparent, you may have to go out looking for them. Joanne Brundage, founder of Formerly Employed Mothers At the Leading Edge (F.E.M.A.L.E.), didn't know any other at-home moms when she decided to quit work. She put an ad in the local newspaper, asking anyone who was at home and interested in mutual support to come meet at her house. Three women showed up that first night, but the group grew until it is now a national organization with chapters in nearly every state.

Peers also include work colleagues. Especially if you work at home, you need a network of other home-working entrepreneurs to banish the isolation, help you problem-solve, and spread the news of your business. The Resources list a number of organizations you can contact.

Other sources of a network of peers might be professional organizations (good to join even if you're not active in your career), home schooling networks, parenting groups, church-sponsored groups. If there is an area of your life you either feel isolated in (perhaps you're the only one you know who home schools), or you want to expand (as when you are ready to get back into the workplace), look for others in your area who are doing the same thing and band together.

2. Mentors. Mentors are another important part of your network. Scripture talks of the importance of teaching older women to train younger women how to be good wives and mothers (Titus 2:3–5). This suggests we younger women don't automatically know how to love our children and husbands—and I think Paul was right!

We need *mentors*—women who are more mature than we, in every area of our lives: women who are more mature spiritually, women who are good wives (if we're married), women whose mothering style we respect and want to emulate. We need women as mentors in our work lives: women who are using their gifts in a similar arena to what we are exploring, whether it be community work, church work, or work in a particular field.

I have consciously cultivated relationships with older women who are more mature than I, who can teach me not only by word but mostly by example what a mature woman of God, wife, and mother looks like. I have found them through church, at work, and even in books. I don't always necessarily ask a person to be my mentor; it's more a matter of cultivating the relationship and watching who they are. Of course, it's usually not all receiving on my part; I try to give, too. But I think there is an implicit recognition that I have more to learn from my mentors than vice versa, and that is fine with them. What they want from the relationship is feedback on my own growth, and that is usually reward enough.

3. People who benefit from our gifts. If with mentors we receive more than give, the situation is reversed with this third group. We need to be cultivating a network of those people who can benefit from our gifts. This circle may be very wide or relatively narrow at this point. Much depends on your design and your present circumstances. If you're an Introvert, for instance, you may have a smaller network, but you may be very important to those few people. If you are a mother at home with young children, those who benefit from your gifts may well be your family, perhaps your children's friends, and/or a small handful of other moms to whom you are a mentor, and that's it. Or it may be a group for whom you volunteer, or the school. Much depends on your own design and energy level.

This third network is made up of people to whom you mostly give. I believe that if you are married with children, as those children grow it is natural to expect your sphere of influence to widen. If that isn't happening, perhaps you are not taking enough risks, trying enough new things. As we grow, we need to look beyond ourselves and our comfort to the world and its many needs. We should consciously reach out to become mentors of younger women. We can be looking for ways to let others know and benefit from our skills and knowledge, personally and professionally.

I am disturbed by the number of women who have taken time out from their careers to raise children and then find that employers belittle those years at home and say that all these women are qualified for are low-skilled jobs. If this is your situation and you are dissatisfied, I urge you to look for other opportunities to gain confidence and expertise in some area that interests you. Check out the resources at the end of this book. The world needs your skills, your wisdom!

A Lifelong Process

That is true for all of us: The world needs everything we've gained through our living. Whatever your design, whatever your circumstances, I'm convinced you have much to give the world. Do not be discouraged if you feel you have made mistakes, or you feel there are no options for you. I believe there are always options if we pray and open ourselves up to them. We must be patient, however, and take one step at a time.

Designing a life you can love takes time. *It is a process.* Most of the women I interviewed who have created options for themselves did so over a period of time. The more they learned of their design (which in itself is an ongoing process), the more they practiced the life skills mentioned in this chapter, the more confident and skilled they became in generating options, and the more those options matched their design.

So start where you are. It doesn't matter where—just *start!* Begin to explore your design, test an interest, hone a skill, make a decision, risk joining a new organization. For a woman, this is both an exciting and frustrating time to be alive. As we seek opportunities to obey the Lord Jesus Christ by using the gifts he's given us in the circumstances in which he's placed us, I believe he will do great things through us. "Do you see a [woman] skilled in [her] work? [She] will serve before kings; [she] will not serve before obscure men" (Prov. 22:29).

Designing a life you can love is a lifelong task, one meant to serve the larger purpose we all share: to know God, to serve him through using our gifts, and to enjoy forever our relationships with him and those he has given us to love.

$\mathcal{A}$PPENDIX A

GENERAL CHARACTERISTICS AND MOTHERING STYLES OF THE SIXTEEN PERSONALITY TYPES

In chapter 2, you explored your "personal style," or preferences in four different areas. In type talk, the four pairs of preferences combine to form a particular type, made up of four letters: E or I (Extraversion or Introversion), S or N (Sensing or iNtuition), T or F (Thinking or Feeling), J or P (Judging or Perceiving). Each of the four preferences work together to form a special dynamic, so that each type has distinct characteristics that set it apart from other types. This section will give you a little more information on each of the sixteen types, and affirm the strengths that come with each in terms of general characteristics and mothering style.

I am grateful to the Center for Applications of Psychological Type (CAPT) for the information on general characteristics taken from *People Types and Tiger Stripes*[1] and to Janet Penley for the information on mothering styles.[2] Descriptions of these highly recommended books upon which the descriptions are based can be found in the Resources section.

ENFJ (Extraversion, iNtuition, Feeling, Judging)

General Characteristics: Imaginative HARMONIZER and worker-with-people; sociable, expressive, orderly, opinionated, conscientious; curious about new ideas and possibilities.

Mothering Style: Expressive and warm, the ENFJ mother is adept at talking about personal concerns, both her children's and her own. She is likely to initiate heart-to-heart talks frequently and provide her children with an open forum for articulating their feelings and perspectives.

Tuned in to each child as a unique person, the ENFJ mother nurtures her children through affirmation, praise, and encouragement. She takes particular pleasure when they reciprocate, offering their admiration and encouragement of her, a sibling, or friend.

Organized and energetic, the ENFJ mother is a competent, efficient family manager. She is involved in her children's lives, providing structure, direction, and guidance.

The ENFJ mother is also socially adept, relating well to people wherever she goes. She strives to keep her children connected to family, neighborhood, and the larger community.

INFJ (Introversion, iNtuition, Feeling, Judging)

General Characteristics: People-oriented HARMONIZER of ideas; serious, quietly forceful and persevering; concerned with the common good, with helping others develop.

Mothering Style: Sensitive and family-focused, the INFJ mother looks for and encourages the unique potential of each child. Self-knowledge may be her byword. Her aim is to help each child develop a sense of who he or she really is and cultivate personal growth. In fact, she may value the mothering experience as a catalyst to her own personal growth and self-knowledge.

The INFJ mother spends time observing and understanding each child. She is drawn to intimate conversations and seeks a free exchange of feelings and thoughts.

Sympathetic and accommodating, the INFJ mother strives to meet the important yet sometimes conflicting needs of each family member in harmonious and creative ways.

She is conscientious and intense as well. Probably no one takes life and child raising more seriously than the INFJ. She approaches mothering as a profession requiring her best self.

ENFP (Extraversion, iNtuition, Feeling, Perceiving)

General Characteristics: Warmly enthusiastic PLANNER OF CHANGE; imaginative, individualistic; pursues inspiration with impulsive energy; seeks to understand and inspire others.

Mothering Style: Playful and energetic, the ENFP mother finds her children good company and enjoys being with them. In fact, she says being with children justifies her own "being a kid again." And children say she's fun to be with—spontaneous, hearty, and imaginative.

Naturally drawn to introducing her children to the joys of life, the ENFP is something of a free spirit. She is less concerned with rules, routines, and schedules, and more inclined to give her children plenty of free time to play, explore on their own or with her, and have fun together.

Tuned in to her children, the ENFP mother enthusiastically encourages each one's individuality and unique potential through a great variety of experiences. She is also quick to identify with others' feelings and thoughts, making her an empathetic supporter of her children . . . not to mention her mate and many, many friends.

INFP (Introversion, iNtuition, Feeling, Perceiving)

General Characteristics: Imaginative, independent HELPER; reflective, inquisitive, empathic, loyal to ideals; more interested in possibilities than practicalities.

Mothering Style: Aware, astute, and understanding, the INFP mother is sensitive to her child's needs, feelings, and perceptions. By observing and listening to the cues of the whole child, she is "tuned in" and naturally develops an intuitive feel for what he or she needs. Responsive and helpful as well, she tends patiently to those needs as they arise.

The INFP mother is comfortable letting her children follow their own course of development and making their own choices. She offers encouragement and uses her insights to head off trouble and/or difficult issues when she can.

The INFP mother takes vicarious pleasure introducing her children to good experiences and watching them enjoy their childhood. She's happiest when creating pleasant, memorable times for the whole family.

ENTJ (Extraversion, iNtuition, Thinking, Judging)

General Characteristics: Intuitive, innovative ORGANIZER; aggressive, analytic, systematic; more tuned to new ideas and possibilities than to people's feelings.

Mothering Style: Competent and confident in a management role, the ENTJ mother organizes the needs and schedules of family members into a workable family system. Within the system, she provides her children with care taking, direction, and limits, but she also gives them the space they need to develop their own self-sufficiency and judgment.

Analytical and adept at problem solving, the ENTJ mother listens to her children's concerns empathetically and then strategizes with them how to improve the situation—either by intervening on their behalf or backing off to let them solve problems on their own. She particularly enjoys watching them take responsibility and accomplish something important to them.

Intense and insightful, the ENTJ mother is cued in to her children's intellectual and emotional development. She uses her quickness and communication skills to talk things through and help her children connect with people and better understand life.

INTJ (Introversion, iNtuition, Thinking, Judging)

General Characteristics: Logical, critical, decisive INNOVATOR of ideas; serious, intent, highly independent, concerned with organization, determined, and often stubborn.

Mothering Style: Individualistic and independent, the INTJ mother is both a role model and teacher of how to be an individual and live life with integrity. She is introspective, defining her own success from within, and generally confident in her decisions. She is unlikely to be persuaded by her children saying "but all the other mothers are doing it."

The INTJ mother is competent in providing for her children's basic needs, but she is likely more focused on developing their self-esteem and confidence. Observant and insightful, she puts great importance on independent thinking and self-efficiency, yet she is comfortable providing protection and boundaries.

Self-motivated and intense, the INTJ works hard and takes life seriously. As a mother, she lives for those moments where she can impart knowledge and offer her children perspectives on life and important issues.

ENTP (Extraversion, iNtuition, Thinking, Perceiving)

General Characteristics: Inventive, analytical PLANNER OF CHANGE; enthusiastic and independent; pursues inspiration with impulsive energy; seeks to understand and inspire others.

Mothering Style: Full of energy and confident in her own self-sufficiency and competence, the ENTP mother encourages her children—as a role model and as a teacher to be independent and confident on their own in the world.

A "big picture" person, she points out options and possibilities along the way. Objective and logical as well, the ENTP wants her children to evaluate their choices and learn from the consequences of their own decisions.

The ENTP mother is resourceful and action-oriented. She likes going places and doing things with her children, exploring all that life has to offer. She is less concerned with rules, routines, and schedules. Introducing her children to new concepts and activities, challenging them, and stimulating their intellectual development are top priorities.

INTP (Introversion, iNtuition, Thinking, Perceiving)

General Characteristics: Inquisitive ANALYZER; reflective, independent, curious; more interested in organizing ideas than situations or people.

Mothering Style: Intellectually curious and patient, the INTP mother relishes those times with a child when they are learning something interesting together. Whether they're at the zoo or computer terminal, she sparks to answering his or her "whys" with in-depth responses or new knowledge.

The INTP mother is also objective and introspective. She listens to and discusses children's ideas and questions as she would a peer, fostering self-esteem and confidence. Open and non-directive, she allows children the freedom to do things for themselves and quietly encourages them to believe they can do it.

Independence, autonomy, intellectual development, and self-reliance are probably the INTP's highest priorities for her children. An avid reader, she naturally imparts an appreciation and love of reading as well.

Drawn to all types of learning, the INTP may also value her mothering experience for all the new insights about life it provides her.

ESTJ (Extraversion, Sensing, Thinking, Judging)

General Characteristics: Fact-minded, practical ORGANIZER; aggressive, analytic, systematic; more interested in getting the job done than in people's feelings.

Mothering Style: Organized and comfortable being in charge, the ESTJ mother knows "how to" get things done, make things happen, and accomplish much on behalf of her children. Whether she is encouraging them to get involved in organized activities or talking with them about their personal concerns, children of the ESTJ mother learn "how to" succeed in life. In many ways, she personifies the American ESTJ culture.

Upbeat and matter-of-fact, the ESTJ mother is directly involved in her children's lives. She is happiest when her efforts produce concrete results—children who try out for teams, participate in academic competitions, play leadership roles among their peers, and can effectively problem-solve.

The ESTJ mother is intent on her children having the best and wants to enhance their experiences. She puts her skills and talents to work to this end, from planning trips that supplement their studies to raising funds for new playground equipment.

The ESTJ mother runs a tight household. She is apt to have predictable expectations, consistent routines, standard procedures, and well-defined boundaries, all of which help her children feel protected and secure.

ISTJ (Introversion, Sensing, Thinking, Judging)

General Characteristics: Analytical MANAGER OF FACTS AND DETAILS; dependable, decisive, painstaking and systematic; concerned with systems and organization; stable and conservative.

Mothering Style: The ISTJ mother has a highly developed sense of responsibility: for work, home, family . . . particularly her children. Whether she's overseeing daily baths or insisting on a 10:00 P.M. curfew, her efforts are largely focused on providing her children with order and routine. She wants them, regardless of age, to be able to count on her and the structure she provides.

In carrying out her commitment to her responsibilities, the ISTJ mother is organized, industrious, and detail-oriented. Because her focus is in the day-to-day realities of life, her children are likely to feel secure and well provided for.

The ISTJ mother also sets a good example and provides her children with practical guidance on being a productive, responsible individual. Still, with all her seriousness, she may delight family members with her quick wit and observations about the details of life.

ESFJ (Extraversion, Sensing, Feeling, Judging)

General Characteristics: Practical HARMONIZER and worker-with-people; sociable, orderly, opinionated, conscientious, realistic, and well-tuned to the here and now.

Mothering Style: The ESFJ mother has a highly developed sense of family and what it takes to be happy in life. Capable and personally invested, she strives to create a happy family where togetherness and harmony flourish. Whether it's taking her children to the park or putting on a holiday feast, her efforts are directed toward everyone's being "happy together."

To many, the ESFJ personifies motherhood. She promotes traditional values, tends to the practical and domestic, provides the family with order and structure, and is directly involved with her children's day-to-day living. The ESFJ mother is a "doer," and she's never happier than when she's "doing" for her family.

Believing the home is central to family life, the ESFJ mother excels at creating an atmosphere that is attractive and offers security.

Energetic and people-oriented, she is drawn to community and the social scene. She helps her children discover the joys of people and groups.

ISFJ (Introversion, Sensing, Feeling, Judging)

General Characteristics: Sympathetic MANAGER OF FACTS AND DETAILS; concerned with people's welfare; dependable, painstaking, and systematic; stable and conservative.

Mothering Style: Gentle and kind, the ISFJ mother provides her children with generous amounts of tenderness, affection, and the comfort of daily routine. Her aim is to "be there" for her children, physically and emotionally. She is sensitive to their feelings, offering closeness, understanding, and quiet support.

Loyal and devoted, the ISFJ mother has a strong sense of duty and consistently puts her children's needs first. She delights in taking care of the little things that matter to a child, making each one feel loved and special.

To provide her family with security and warmth, the ISFJ mother tends to the practical and domestic, aiming for a smooth-running household and attractive home. She also observes and conveys the importance of family traditions.

ESTP (Extraversion, Sensing, Thinking, Perceiving)

General Characteristics: REALISTIC ADAPTER in the world of material things; good-natured, tolerant, easygoing; oriented to practical, firsthand experience; highly observant of details of things.

Mothering Style: Active and spontaneous, the ESTP mother can turn ordinary life into a fun-filled adventure. She makes dull routines exciting and chores a "let's do it again" kind of game. Her best times are those spent with her children actively doing, particularly if it's spur of the moment, innovative, and even a little crazy.

Full of energy and enthusiasm for living in the moment, the ESTP mother gives her children every opportunity to experience all that life has to offer—touching, seeing, moving, doing . . . and people. She's interested in stimulating all the senses so they can take life in and live it.

The ESTP mother is matter-of-fact—"what you see is what you get." She mothers without hidden agendas and takes life and people as they are. Her children know where they stand. She is able to develop a close relationship with them based on honesty and a strong family-orientation as well as sharing a wide variety of experiences.

ISTP (Introversion, Sensing, Thinking, Perceiving)

General Characteristics: Practical ANALYZER; values exactness; more interested in organizing data than situations or people; reflective, a cool and curious observer of life.

Mothering Style: Nonintrusive and respectful of differences, the ISTP mother gives her children the personal space they need to develop as separate, self-sufficient individuals. As each child grows and matures, she enjoys observing how he or she becomes his or her own person. She seeks to accept and honor each one's interests, opinions, and choices.

The ISTP mother does not believe in authority or control for its own sake. Instead, she favors a nondirective approach. Yet she has high expectations for each child's self-discipline . . . as a key to self-sufficiency.

To these ends, the ISTP mother wants to "be there" for her children—to meet their basic needs and keep them safe. Her goal as a mother is to help her children think for themselves and take responsibility for their own actions.

ESFP (Extraversion, Sensing, Feeling, Perceiving)

General Characteristics: REALISTIC ADAPTER in human relationships; friendly and easy with people, highly observant of their feelings and needs; oriented to practical, firsthand experience.

Mothering Style: Energetic and people-oriented, the ESFP mother lives in the moment, "totally there" for her children—totally focused on them when she is with them. She enjoys being with her children and can respond to their needs "on the spot," ensuring they feel loved and cared for.

Fun-loving, friendly, and outgoing, the ESFP mother actively engages her children in a wide variety of experiences. They can count on her to strike up a conversation with a fellow shopper at the market or with the UPS driver, introducing them to the joys of people everywhere.

Devoted and practical, the ESFP mother also enjoys doing things for her children. She is attentive to their feelings and is deeply touched by every joy or hurt they experience.

ISFP (Introversion, Sensing, Feeling, Perceiving)

General Characteristics: Observant, loyal HELPER; reflective, realistic, empathic; patient with details, gentle and retiring; shuns disagreements; enjoys the moment.

Mothering Style: Quiet and unassuming in her devotion, the ISFP mother is responsive to her children's needs, offering behind-the-scenes love and support. She is gentle and nonintrusive, flexible and adaptable.

A "be there" mother, the ISFP takes pleasure in physically caring for her children and doing for them. Her best times might be "doing little things" with each child one-on-one.

More than anything, the ISFP mother wants her children to know they are loved, and she enjoys being needed in return.

Dedicated to raising children who are responsible and care for others, she favors a nondirective approach: instilling values by setting a good example. She may be a strong role model for community service.

$\mathscr{A}$PPENDIX B

RESOURCES

On Work and Decision-Making

Bolles, Richard. *The Three Boxes of Life and How to Get Out of Them*. Berkeley: Ten Speed Press, 1978.

The "three boxes" are education, work, and recreation; Bolles helps us to integrate all of these in every period of our lives, rather than spend decades concentrating on only one to the neglect of the other two. Good perspective for those in an employment crisis.

Friesen, Garry, with J. Robin Mason. *Decision Making and the Will of God*. Portland, OR: Multnomah Press, 1980.

Help for anyone struggling to understand how to know God's will.

Harris, Janis Long. *Secrets of People Who Love Their Work*. Downers Grove, IL: InterVarsity Press, 1992.

Based on interviews with people who love their work, Janis Long Harris explores how to discover one's "gifted passions" in work.

Sherman, Doug, and William Hendricks. *Your Work Matters to God*. Colorado Springs: NavPress, 1987.

For anyone who wants to gain a biblical perspective on work.

Sinetar, Marsha. *Do What You Love, the Money Will Follow: Discovering Your Right Livelihood*. New York: Paulist Press, 1987.

The title says it all; Sinetar wants to inspire us to find work we love, to find our "calling." Yes!

White, Jerry, and Mary White. *Your Job: Survival or Satisfaction? Christian Discipleship in a Secular Job*. Grand Rapids, MI: Zondervan, 1977.

Looks at work from a larger, Christian perspective and discusses ways to find greater satisfaction no matter what the job is.

On Working and Mothering

Crosby, Faye. *Juggling: The Unexpected Advantages of Balancing Career and Home for Women and Their Families*. New York: MacMillan, Inc., 1991.

Especially helpful for those working full-time. However, I was personally bothered by the chapter called, "What about the Children?" I thought that chapter never really answered the question and glossed over some very important considerations.

Dynerman, Susan Bacon, and Lynn O'Rourke Hayes. *The Best Jobs in America for Parents Who Want Careers and Time for Children Too*. New York: Rawson Assoc., 1991.

Eyre, Linda, and Richard Eyre. *Lifebalance: Priority Balance, Attitude Balance, Goal Balance in All Areas of Your Life*. New York: Ballantine Books, 1987.

Linamen, Karen Scalf, and Linda Holland. *Working Women, Workable Lives: Creative Solutions for Managing Home and Career*. Carol Stream, IL: Harold Shaw Publishers, 1993.

Michaels, Bonnie, and Elizabeth McCarty. *Solving the Work/Family Puzzle*. Homewood, IL: Business One Irwin, 1992.

Exhaustive look at all the questions that come up; also deals with elder care.

Neff, Miriam. *Working Moms: From Survival to Satisfaction*. Colorado Springs: NavPress, 1992.

A balanced Christian perspective on working and mothering.

Sanger, Sirgay, and John Kelly. *The Woman Who Works, the Parent Who Cares*. Boston: Little, Brown and Co., 1987. Especially helpful for the woman who works full-time.

On Personality Types

Brownsword, Alan. *It Takes All Types!* San Alselmo, CA: Baytree Publications Company, 1987.

Keirsey, David, and Marilyn Bates. *Please Understand Me: Character and Temperament Types.* Del Mar, CA: Prometheus Nemesis, 1978.

This popular book about temperaments includes a short "type sorter."

Kroeger, Otto, and Janet M. Thuesen, *Type Talk: How to Determine Your Personality Type and Change Your Life.* New York: Delacorte Books, 1988.

A thorough introduction to type theory as it applies to work and relationships, with comprehensive descriptions of the sixteen types.

Lawrence, Gordon. *People Types and Tiger Stripes: A Practical Guide to Learning Styles,* 2d. ed. Gainesville, FL: Center for Applications of Psychological Type, 1982.

Although this was written for teachers, I found it helpful as a parent. The author describes the types clearly and gives practical suggestions for working with children of different types. Includes an early version of Isabel Myers' *Introduction to Type.*

Myers, Isabel Briggs. *Introduction to Type: A Description of the Theory and Application of the Myers-Briggs Type Indicator,* 5th ed. Palo Alto, CA: Consulting Psychologists Press, 1993.

The best, most readable introduction to type available.

Myers, Isabel Briggs, with Peter B. Myers, *Gifts Differing.* Palo Alto, CA: Consulting Psychologists Press, 1980.

This book was written by one of the developers of the MBTI and is highly recommended for its readability and accuracy.

Neff, LaVonne. *One of a Kind: Making the Most of Your Child's Uniqueness.* Gainesville, FL: Center for Applications of Psychological Type, 1994.

Talks about type as it relates to raising children.

Penley, Janet, and Diane Stephens. *Mothers of Many Styles®.* Wilmette, IL: Penley & Associates, 604 Maple Avenue,

Wilmette, Illinois 60091; (708) 251–4936, 1994.

Looks at how personality type affects mothering styles, with tips for how to maximize strengths and minimize stress.

Tieger, Paul D., and Barbara Barron-Tieger. *Do What You Are: Discover the Perfect Career for You Through the Secrets of Personality Type.* Boston: Little, Brown and Company, 1992.

Very readable, thorough look at how to maximize your type's strengths in your career.

On Skills Assessments

Books

Bradley, John, and Jay Carty. *Unlocking Your Sixth Suitcase.* Colorado Springs: NavPress, 1991.

Haldane, Bernard. *Career Satisfaction and Success: How to Know and Manage Your Strengths*, Revised Edition. New York: AMACOM.

Now available through Bernard Haldane, Wellness Education Council, 4502 54th NW, Seattle, WA 98105.

Jones, Gordon, and Rosemary Jones. *Naturally Gifted: A Self-Discovery Workbook.* Downers Grove, IL: InterVarsity Press, 1993.

Miller, Arthur F., and Ralph T. Mattson. *The Truth About You.* Berkeley, CA: Ten Speed Press, 1989.

All of these four books take you step-by-step through a process of discovering innate abilities and motivations and relating this self-knowledge to the world of work. Any of them are good expansions of what I've given you in chapter 3. Haldane's was the original and also contains some very useful goal-setting and career-building strategies.

On Mothering

Baumbich, Charlene Ann. *Don't Miss Your Kids.* Downers Grove, IL: InterVarsity Press, 1991.

A wonderfully warm and wise book that will remind you of what it means to *enjoy* your kids.

Block, Joyce. *Motherhood As Metamorphosis*. New York: The Penguin Group, 1990.

Converse, Kimberly, and Richard Hagstrom. *The Myth of the Perfect Mother*. Eugene, OR: Harvest House, 1993.

Harris, Janis Long. *What Good Parents Have in Common*. Grand Rapids, MI: Zondervan, 1994.

Based on more than fifty interviews with people who felt their parents did a good job, this book looks at thirteen secrets of good parenting—some of which will surprise you.

Lewis, Deborah Shaw. *Motherhood Stress*. Grand Rapids, MI: Zondervan, 1992.

Identifies the many sources of motherhood stress and gives practical tips for coping.

Newenhuyse, Elizabeth Cody. *Sometimes I Feel Like Running Away from Home*. Minneapolis, MN: Bethany House, 1993.

Stories and encouragement from someone who has been there.

For Stay-at-Home Mothers

Books

Barr, Debbie. *A Season at Home: The Joy of Fully Sharing Your Child's Critical Years*. Grand Rapids, MI: Zondervan, 1993.

Excellent resource guide for those wanting to make this choice, from a Christian perspective.

Cardozo, Arlene Rossen. *Sequencing: Having It All But Not All at Once*. New York: Atheneum, 1986.

Davidson, Christine. *Staying Home Instead: Alternatives to the Two-Paycheck Family*, revised and expanded edition. New York: MacMillan, Inc., 1993.

Hunter, Brenda. *Home by Choice*. Portland, OR: Multnomah Press, 1991.

Contains a wealth of research to validate this choice.

Sanders, Darcie, and Bullen, Martha. *Staying Home: From Full-Time Professional to Full-Time Parent*. Boston: Little, Brown and Company, 1992.

Very thorough and readable look at how to make the transition.

Support Groups

F.E.M.A.L.E. (Formerly Employed Mothers At the Leading Edge), P.O. Box 31, Elmhurst, IL 60126; (708) 941–3553.

Has local chapters across the country and publishes a newsletter (annual membership: $20).

MOPS International (Mothers of Preschoolers), 1311 South Clarkson Street, Denver, CO 80210; (303) 733–5353.

A Christian ministry to mothers of children under kindergarten age. Publishes a monthly newsletter and has chartered groups in churches across the country.

Mothers At Home, 8310A Old Courthouse Road, Vienna, VA 22181.

The monthly magazine, *Welcome Home*, provides a forum for at-home Moms and represents mothers at home to the media and government. Magazine subscription: $15 per year.

La Leche League, 1–800-LA-LECHE (800) 525–3243.

Provides support and information for breast-feeding mothers and a bimonthly magazine, *New Beginnings* (subscription: $15).

On Saving Money

Dacyczyn, Amy. *The Tightwad Gazette*. New York: Villard Books, 1993 and *The Tightwad Gazette II*, 1995..

This is also the name of a monthly newsletter, available for $12 per year's subscription, from *Tightwad Gazette*, RR1 Box 3570, Leeds, Maine 04263.

Freebie Magazine: The Magazine with Something for Nothing, P.O. Box 20283, Santa Barbara, CA 93120; (805) 962–9135. Good for getting things for kids.

Gallagher, Patricia. *Raising Happy Kids on a Reasonable Budget*. Cincinnati, OH: Better Way Books, 1993.

Globe Pequot Press, 10 Denlar Drive, P.O. Box Q, Chester, CT 06412; (203) 526–4930.

Call or write for their free catalog listing budget-minded books on a variety of topics.

Goldstein, Sue. *The Complete Home Shopper*. New York: McGraw-Hill, 1989. Also, *Guide to Off-Price Shopping*.

Hatton, Hap, and Laura Torbet. *Helpful Hints for Hard Times: How to Live It Up While Cutting Down*. New York: Facts on File Publications, 1983.

Hunt, Mary. *The Best of the Cheap-Skate Monthly*. New York: St. Martin's Press, 1993.

Simple tips for living frugally, from the newsletter.

Leonard, Walter B., and the editors of Consumer Reports Books. *Money-Saving Tips for Good Times and Bad*. Yonkers, New York: Consumer Reports Books, 1992.

Sorenson, Stephen, and Amanda Sorenson. *Living Smart, Spending Less*. Chicago: Moody Press, 1993.

Chock-full of practical ways to save money in every area. I especially like the attitude they convey—that saving money can be a lot of fun. There is also a workbook.

Woods, R. *Consumer Information Catalog*, Consumer Information Center–3A, P.O. Box 100, Pueblo, CO 81002.

Free catalog offers pamphlets on lowering auto insurance, buying surplus personal property from the Department of Defense, and growing vegetables in your garden. May be available at your public library. Pamphlets are free or for a nominal cost.

On Working from Home
Books

Alarid, William, and Gustav Berle. *Free Help from Uncle Sam to Start Your Own Business*. Puma Publishing, 1670 Voral Dr., Santa Maria, CA 93454.

Arden, Lynie. *The Work-at-Home Sourcebook: How to Find "At Home" Work That's Right for You*. Boulder, CO: Live Oak Publications, 1987.

Christensen, Kathleen. *Women and Home-Based Work: The Unspoken Contract*. New York: Henry Holt and Company, 1988.

A realistic look at what it takes to work from home successfully.

Hall, Daryl Allen. *1001 Businesses You Can Start from Home: The World's Most Complete Directory of Part-Time and Full-Time Business Ideas, Including Start-up Costs, Marketing Tips, Sources of Information*. New York: John Wiley & Sons, Inc., 1992.

Edwards, Paul, and Sarah Edwards. *Working from Home*. Los Angeles: Jeremy P. Tarcher, Inc., 1990.

A very practical, comprehensive, and readable book that covers just about everything you need to know about starting, maintaining, and succeeding at a home-based business.

Kamoroff, Bernard. *Small-Time Operator*. Laytonville, CA: Bell Springs Publishing.

Revised and updated yearly. Practical workbook for building a business around your interests (written by a CPA).

Karlson, David. *Consulting for Success: A Guide for Prospective Consultants*. Los Altos, CA: Crispt Publications, 1991.

Workbook format, covers how to become an independent consultant, selling your skills on a contract basis.

Kern, Coralee Smith, and Tammara Hoffman Wolfgram. *How to Run Your Own Home Business*. Lincolnwood, IL: VGM Career Horizons, 1990.

Takes you from deciding if you're suited to working at home, to how to select a business, set it up, and keep it going. Includes several worksheets.

Partow, Donna. *Homemade Business: A Woman's Step-By-Step Guide to Earning Money at Home*. Colorado Springs: Focus on the Family, 1992.

Sheedy, Edna. *Start and Run a Profitable Home-Based Business*. Bellingham, WA: Self-Counsel Press, 1990.

Periodicals and Newsletters

Home Office Computing magazine, 740 Broadway, New York, NY 10003.

This sounds like it's just for computer buffs, but it's really chock-full of helpful information to almost anyone who works from home. A one-year subscription costs $19.97.

Entrepreneur: The Small Business Authority, and *New Business Opportunities: The Business Start-Up Magazine,* 2392 Morse Avenue, Irvine, CA 92714.

Working Options, Crescent Plaza, Suite 216, 7700 Leesburg Pike, Falls Church, VA 22043; (703) 734–7975.

A newsletter published by the Association of Part-Time Professionals.

Organizations and Contacts

American Federation of Small Business (AFSB), 407 S. Dearborn St., Chicago, IL 60605–115; (312) 427–0207.

American Home Business Association (AHBA), 397 Post Rd., Darien, CT 06820; (203) 655–4380.

American Small Business Association (ASBA), P.O. Box 612663, Dallas, TX 75261; (800) 880–2722.

American Women's Economic Development Corporation (AWED), 641 Lexington Ave., New York, NY 10022; (800) 222-AWED. In Hawaii, Alaska, and New York City, (212) 688–1900.

Offers professional consultation by telephone 10:00 A.M. to 5:00 P.M. (EST); $10 for hotline, $35 for business counseling. Also offices in Washington, D.C. and Los Angeles: AWED, 301 W. Ocean Blvd., Long Beach, CA 90802; (213) 983–3747.

Mother's Home Business Network (MHBN), P.O. Box 423, East Meadow, NY 11554–0423; (516) 997–7394.

Send SASE for information and list of publications.

National Association for Family Day Care, 725 Fifteenth St., N.W., Suite 505, Washington, D.C. 20005; (800) 359–3817.

Send SASE for information on how to start a family day care business.

National Association for the Self-Employed (NASE), P.O. Box 612067, DFW Airport, TX 75261; (800) 232–6273.

National Association of Women Business Owners (NAWBO), 600 S. Federal, Chicago, IL 60605; (312) 922–6222.

Offers advice on networking and conferences.

National Business Association (NBA), 14875 Landmark Blvd., Suite 100, Dallas, TX 75240; (800) 456–0440.

National Federation of Independent Business (NFIB), 150 W. 20th Ave., San Mateo, CA 94430.

The National Independent Business League, (800) 683–0575.

On Part-Time, Flexible, and Job-Share Work Options
Books

Canape, Charlene. *The Part-Time Solution.* New York: Harper & Row, 1990.

Good book on managing career and motherhood at the same time.

Olmsted, Barney, and Suzanne Smith. *The Job-Sharing Handbook.* Berkeley, CA: Ten Speed Press, 1983.

Everything you need to know about this option, written by pioneers in the field.

Rothberg, Diane S., and Barbara Ensor Cook. *Part-Time Professional.* Washington, D.C.: Acropolis Books, Ltd., 1985.

Examples of women who are professional part-timers and how they did it, plus lots of practical tips.

Organizations and Contacts

Association of Part-Time Professionals, P.O. Box 3419, Alexandria, VA 22302; (703) 734–7975.

Write to them for the Part-Timer's Resource Kit.

New Ways to Work, 149 Ninth St., San Francisco, CA 94103; (415) 552–1000.

On Developing Job-hunting Skills
Books

Baker, Wayne E. *Networking Smart: How to Build Relationships for Personal and Organizational Success.* New York: McGraw-Hill, Inc., 1994.

Excellent book on smart networking. No matter what you are

doing now, you will find this book helpful.

Bloomberg, Gerri, and Margaret Holden. *The Women's Job Search Handbook*. Charlotte, VT: Williamson Publishing, 1991.

Deals specifically with issues related to women's job search.

Bolles, Richard. *What Color Is Your Parachute?* Berkeley, CA: Ten Speed Press, revised annually.

The leading best-seller on finding a job, and my perennial favorite for its completeness, warm and readable tone, and perspective. The 1994 version is very different from the earlier editions; in it Bolles discusses the major changes in the job market in these recent years and adapts his approach to those who want to change careers as well as choose a career. But earlier editions contain his Quick Job-Hunting Map (also available separately) and (since 1989) a very helpful section on "finding your mission in life."

Ellis, Lee, and Larry Burkett. *Your Career in Changing Times*. Chicago, IL: Moody Press, 1993.

Also, the companion workbook, *Finding the Career That Fits You*.

Figler, Howard. *The Complete Job-Search Handbook*, revised and expanded edition. New York: Henry Holt and Company, 1988.

Looks at the skills you need to get any job, and tries to help you enjoy the job hunt as well.

Germann, Richard, and Peter Arnold. *Bernard Haldane Associates' Job and Career Building*. Berkeley, CA: Ten Speed Press, 1980.

This is for someone who already knows what she wants to do; gives specific details on how to find the job you want. Especially helpful for executives. Adapted from Bernard Haldane Associates' well-known program.

Haldane, Bernard. *Career Satisfaction and Success: How to Know and Manage Your Strengths*. Wellness Behavior, Seattle, WA: 4502 54th Avenue, NE, Seattle, WA 98105, 1988.

Insights from a man who fathered the whole concept of looking at past achievements for future direction.

Half, Robert. *How to Get a Better Job in This Crazy World*. New York: Crown Publishers, 1990.

The author emphasizes the necessity of learning and keeping on top of developments in your field and in the work world. Readable, often humorous tone.

Irish, Richard K. *Go Hire Yourself an Employer*. Revised and expanded edition. New York: Anchor Press/Doubleday, 1987.

A practical book about finding what Irish calls a "judgment job"—one you do because you want to do it, which uses your most enjoyable skills and addresses needs in the world at large.

Jackson, Tom. *Guerrilla Tactics in the New Job Market*, second edition. New York: Bantam Books, 1991.

This is a very popular book that has been updated for the 1990s. Some fresh insights and helpful advice.

Kline, Linda, and Lloyd Seinstein. *Career Changing: The Worry-Free Guide*. New York: Little, Brown and Company, 1982.

Very helpful and encouraging workbook on finding new ways to transfer current skills.

Krannich, Ronald I. *Careering and Re-Careering for the 1990s*, second edition. Woodbridge, VA: Impact Publications, 1991.

Very thorough treatment of the current and future job market and the skills, attitudes, and approaches needed to succeed in it. Krannich also coauthored other books on specific job-search skills: *Network Your Way to Job & Career Success, Dynamite Cover Letters & Other Great Job Search Letters, High Impact Resumés & Letters: How to Communicate Your Qualifications to Employers*.

LeCompte, Michelle, ed. *Job Hunter's Sourcebook: Where to Find Employment Leads and Other Job Search Resources*. Detroit: Gale Research, Inc.

Tells you how to find sources of information and job leads for a wide range of occupations.

Lewis, Diane, with Joe Carroll. *The Insider's Guide to Finding the Right Job*. Nashville: Thomas Nelson Publishers, 1987.

An upbeat, easy-to-read, encouraging look at what employers

look for and job-finding techniques.

Nivens, Beatryce. *Careers for Women without College Degrees.* New York: McGraw-Hill, 1988.

Scheele, Adele M. *Skills for Success.* New York: Ballantine Books, 1979.

Scheele studied successful people in all walks of life and identified six "critical career competencies": experiencing doing, risking linking, showing belonging, exhibiting specializing, using catapulting, magnifying accomplishing. Highly recommended.

Sher, Barbara. *Wishcraft: How to Get What You Really Want.* New York: Ballantine Books, 1983.

Very encouraging and inspirational.

Spina, Vicki L. *Getting Hired in the '90s.* Schaumburg, IL: Corporate Image Publishers, 1450 E. American Lane, Suite 1400, Schaumburg, IL 60173.

Includes a money-back guarantee!

Templeton, Mary Ellen. *Help! My Job Interview Is Tomorrow! How to Use the Library to Research an Employer.* New York: Schuman Publishers, 1991.

Written by a university librarian, this workbook shows you how to uncover information about a prospective employer. Includes a bibliography of hundreds of business directories.

Organizations and Contacts

Career Pathways, P.O. Box 1476, Gainesville, GA 30501; (706) 534–1000.

Offers, for a reasonable fee, a comprehensive assessment and help in finding the right career path.

Ingenious Center at Family University, 2120 E. Northwest Highway, Arlington Heights, IL 60004; (708) 392–1858.

This organization will take you through a process something like I describe in chapter 3. They will ask you to come up with a list of Satisfying Activities, interview you, and write up a detailed analysis of your skills, for a fee.

Maximum Potential, P.O. Box 24618, Tempe, AZ 85285–4618; (800) 809–0165.

Offers assessment, a biblically-based perspective on work, and telephone follow-up.

On Finding Child Care

Books

Miller, Jo Ann, and Susan Weissman. *The Parents' Guide to Daycare.* New York: Bantam Books, 1986.

Siegel-Gorelick, Bryna. *The Working Parents' Guide to Day Care.* Boston: Little, Brown and Company, 1983.

Zitzman, Susan M. *All-Day Care: Exploring the Options for You and Your Child.* Wheaton, IL: Harold Shaw Publishers, 1990.

My favorite, because it looks at the needs of children and discusses options both for at-home mothers and employed mothers.

General Information and Referral Agencies

"Finding Good Child Care." For a checklist and other information, send a stamped, self-addressed envelope to Child Care Action Campaign, 330 Seventh Ave., 18th Floor, New York, NY 10001.

"How to Choose a Good Early Childhood Program." Send twenty-five cents to the Chicago Association for the Education of Young Children, 410 S. Michigan Ave., Chicago, IL 60605.

National Association of Child Care Resources and Referral Agencies will help you locate a referral agency in your area. Contact: NACCRRA, 2116 Campus Drive SE, Rochester, MN 55904; (507) 287–2020.

*N*OTES

Chapter 2: A Personal Style You Can Love

1. I first came across the theory of psychological types in a book by David Keirsey and Marilyn Bates called *Please Understand Me*. This theory has provided me some rich understanding into who I am and has helped me appreciate the differences of others.

2. The information on type theory was drawn from the following books: *Gifts Differing* by Isabel Briggs Myers; *Please Understand Me* by David Keirsey and Marilyn Bates; *Type Talk: The 16 Personality Types That Determine How We Live, Love and Work* by Otto Kroeger and Janet M. Thuesen; *Do What You Are* by Paul D. Tieger and Barbara Barron-Tieger; *People Types and Tiger Stripes* by Gordon Lawrence.; *Type Talk* by Otto Kroeger and Janet M. Thuesen; *One of a Kind* by LaVonne Neff; and *Mothers of Many Styles®, A Personalized Profile of Your Mothering Style* by Janet Penley and Diane Stephens. Information on these and other books is given in Appendix B.

3. Janet Penley, and Diane Stephens, *Mothers of Many Styles®, A Personalized Profile of Your Mothering Style* (Wilmette, IL: Penley and Associates, Inc. 1995), 17.

Chapter 3: Discover the Energy of Your Design

1. I am indebted to Bernard Haldane, Richard Bolles, Ralph Mattson, Arthur Miller, and Richard Hagstrom for helping me understand this process of identifying and analyzing satisfying activities.

2. This interview process is adapted from Richard Bolles's suggestions

in *What Color Is Your Parachute?* (Berkeley, CA: Ten Speed Press, 1994), 179, 201.

3. If you are motivated to analyze your satisfying activities in greater detail, I suggest any of the following, which will take you step by step. Books by Richard N. Bolles: *How to Create A Picture of Your Ideal Job or Next Career*, Advanced Version (revised) of the *The Quick Job-Hunting (and Career-Changing) Map*; *The Quick Job-Hunting (and Career-Changing) Map for Beginners*, (Berkeley, CA: Ten Speed Press, Box 7123, Berkeley, CA 94707). Also: Arthur Miller and Ralph Mattson, *The Truth About You: Discover What You Should Be Doing with Your Life* (Berkeley, CA: Ten Speed Press, 1977, 1989); John Bradley and Jay Carty, *Unlocking Your Sixth Suitcase* (Colorado Springs: NavPress, 1991); Gordon and Rosemary Jones, *Naturally Gifted*, (Downers Grove, IL: InterVarsity Press, 1993).

Chapter 4: A Purpose You Can Love

1. Richard N. Bolles, *How to Find Your Mission in Life* (Berkeley, CA: Ten Speed Press, 1991), 31.

2. The term "gifted passions" was coined by Janis Long Harris, in her book *Secrets of People Who Love Their Work* (Downers Grove, IL: InterVarsity Press, 1992).

3. Richard N. Bolles, *How to Find Your Mission in Life,* 41.

4. Quoted from Frederick Buechner, *Wishful Thinking—A Theological ABC*, in Richard N. Bolles, *How to Find Your Mission In Life* (Berkeley, CA: Ten Speed Press, 1991), 48.

5. This idea comes from career counselor Richard Hagstrom, who is coauthor of the books *Discover Your Best Possible Future* (Grand Rapids, MI: Zondervan, 1992) and *The Myth of the Perfect Mother* (Eugene, OR: Harvest House, 1993).

Chapter 5: Designing Your Own Mothering Style

1. Richard Bolles, *What Color Is Your Parachute?*, 1994 edition, (Berkeley, CA: Ten Speed Press, 1994), 203. Used by permission of the author. (Note that I have added "nurturing" and "disciplining.")

2. Adapted from Janet Penley and Diane Stephens, *Mothers of Many Styles®, A Personalized Profile of Your Mothering Style* (Wilmette, IL: Penley and Associates, 1995). Used by permission of Janet Penley.

3. Deborah Shaw Lewis, *Motherhood Stress* (Dallas: Word, 1989), 54–55.

Chapter 6: Sequencing: Designs for the Seasons of Life

1. This outline for making good decisions is based on Isabel Myers' suggestions in *Gifts Differing* (Palo Alto, CA: Consulting Psychologists Press, 1980), 205–6. Note that it takes into account Sensing (to gather the facts), Intuition (to discern possibilities), Thinking (to objectively anticipate probable consequences), and Feeling (to weigh the desirability of each outcome in human terms). Since two of these will be your strong suit, and two will not be, you might want to seek the input of a friend who is strong in your weak areas to help you weigh all the factors.

2. Barr cites several studies done from 1980 to 1991, which focused on the attachment bond between mother and infant. It appears that other-care in the first year of an infant's life disrupts the emotional attachment between mother and child and may predispose children toward temper tantrums, noncompliance, negativism, and lowered enthusiasm when confronting a challenge. See Debbie Barr, *A Season at Home* (Grand Rapids, MI: Zondervan, 1993), 36–9.

3. Barbara Dafoe Whitehead, "The New Family Values," F.E.M.A.L.E. *Forum*, March 1994: 4. Condensed from *FAMILY AFFAIRS*, Summer 1992, Volume V, No. 1–2.

4. Arlene Rossen Cardozo, *Sequencing* (New York: MacMillan, Inc., 1986), 94.

5. To find out if there are local chapters near you, contact F.E.M.A.L.E. at: P.O. Box 31, Elmhurst, IL 60126; (708) 941–3553; MOPS International at 1311 South Clarkson Street, Denver, CO 80210. Other support resources are listed in Appendix B.

6. Darcie Sanders and Martha M. Bullen, *Staying Home: From Full-Time Professional to Full-Time Parent* (Boston: Little, Brown and Company, 1992), 37.

7. Ibid., 33, 35.

Chapter 7: Staying Home—by Design

1. Janet Penley and Diane Stephens, *Mothers of Many Styles®, A Personalized Profile of Your Mothering Style* (Wilmette, IL: Penley and Associates, 1995), 26.

2. Ralph Mattson and Arthur Miller, *Finding a Job You Can Love* (Nashville: Thomas Nelson Publishers, 1982), 134.

Chapter 8: Part-Time and Professional

1. Items one through seven are adapted from Diane S. Rothberg and Barbara Ensor Cook, *Part-Time Professional* (Washington, D.C.: Acropolis Books, 1985), 17–18.

2. Many newspapers and magazines have written about the viability of the so-called "contingency work force"—i.e., part-time workers. Three books that also present a good case for possible employer objections and how to respond, are: Diane S. Rothberg and Barbara Ensor Cook, *Part-Time Professional* (Washington, D.C.: Acropolis Books, 1985); Charlene Canape, *The Part-Time Solution: The New Strategy for Managing Your Career While Managing Motherhood* (New York: Harper & Row, 1990); Bonnie Michaels and Elizabeth McCarty, *Solving the Work/Family Puzzle* (Homewood, IL: Business One Irwin, 1992).

Chapter 9: Working from Home

1. Andrew Leckey, "Home Offices Fit Entrepreneur Era," *Chicago Tribune*, August 1, 1991, Section 3, page 3.

2. This estimate is extrapolated from a survey conducted by Kathleen Christensen, reported in her book *Women and Home-Based Work: The Unspoken Contract* (New York: Henry Holt and Company, 1988), 5. She found that half of her survey respondents who worked exclusively at home were mothers who based their choices on family reasons. Given the trends

in the workplace, it is probable that at least half, if not more, of self-employed women are mothers working from home.

3. Thomas E. Miller, LINK Resources Group in New York, National Work-at-Home Survey, 1987; quoted in Darcie Sanders and Martha Bullen, *Staying Home: From Full-Time Professional to Full-Time Parent* (Boston: Little, Brown and Company, 1992), 11.

4. Kathleen Christensen, interviewed by Laurie Koblesky, "Women and Home-Based Work," F.E.M.A.L.E. *Forum*, April 1990, 4.

5. Christine Davidson, *Staying Home Instead: Alternatives to the Two-Paycheck Family*, revised and expanded edition (New York: MacMillan, Inc., 1993), 131.

Chapter 10: Working Full-Time

1. Kathleen Christensen, *Women and Home-Based Work: The Unspoken Contract* (New York: Henry Holt and Company, 1988), xiii.

2. Amanda Vogt, "Half a Loaf: Flextime Gains Backers, But It's No Avalanche," *Chicago Tribune* (October 3, 1993), Section 6, p. 1.

3. Faye J. Crosby, *Juggling* (New York: The Free Press, 1991), 77.

4. Ibid., 78.

5. Ibid., 8–9.

6. Taken from the paper, "Flexible Work Arrangements," Families and Work Institute, 330 Seventh Avenue, New York, NY 10001.

7. Kenneth Labich, "Can Your Career Hurt Your Kids?" *Fortune* (May 20, 1991), 44.

8. Sarah Hutter, "Flexibility at Work," *Working Mother* (March 1994), 26.

9. You may request this fact sheet, which also includes part-time and job sharing, and gives advantages, disadvantages, and prevalence of each option, by sending a stamped, self-addressed envelope to the address given in footnote 6. You

may also call the Work and Family Clearinghouse of the Women's Bureau in the U.S. Department of Labor at 1–800–827–5335 to request a free "Work and Family Resource Kit."

10. Miriam Neff, *Working Moms: From Survival to Satisfaction* (Colorado Springs: NavPress, 1992), 117–18.

Chapter 11: Taking Charge of Your Life

1. Isabel Briggs Myers, *Introduction to Type*, fifth edition (Palo Alto, CA: Consulting Psychologists Press, Inc., 1993), 29.

2. Ibid.

3. Ibid.

4. Adele Scheele, *Skills for Success* (New York: Ballantine Books, 1979), 37.

5. See Wayne E. Baker, *Networking Smart* (New York: McGraw-Hill, 1994), 189.

Appendix A: General Characteristics and Mothering Styles of the Sixteen Personality Types

1. Gordon Lawrence, *People Types and Tiger Stripes*, 3d ed. (Gainesville, FL: Center for Psychological Types, 1993), 14.

2. Janet Penley and Diane Stephens, *Mothers of Many Styles®, A Personalized Profile of Your Mothering Style* (Wilmette, IL: Penley and Associates, 1995).